Reflections

A YEAR OF RENEWAL, FAITH, AND GRACE

REV . SCOT SAUL

Published by Hemingway Publishers

Cover design by Hemingway Publishers

ISBN: Printed in the United States

Dedication

For everyone who has ever whispered, "Lord, I'm trying." May these pages meet you in real life with real grace.

To my wife Veronica and our daughters you taught me what steady love looks like.

To Rob & Shirley for your unwavering belief

To Jesus the reason for every word.

Acknowledgment

First and foremost, I give thanks to my Lord and Savior, Jesus Christ. Every word written and every truth shared in these pages flows from His grace and goodness. Without Him, there would be no message, there would be only empty pages.

To my wife, whose steadfast faith, compassion, and Spirit-filled life continue to inspire me daily; thank you for walking beside me in ministry and in life. Your love for people and your unwavering support have been a reflection of Christ's love to me and to many others.

To my family & friends, thank you for your encouragement, prayers, and patience as I followed the Lord's prompting to put these devotionals into words.

To those who have walked with us in ministry, our mentors, our friends, our brothers and sisters who serve faithfully, you are living proof of God's hands at work in this world.

And finally, to the readers of these devotionals: may these words draw you nearer to the heart of Jesus. May you come to know not only His saving grace but also the depth of His love that meets you right where you are.

All glory to God, who still speaks, still saves, and still changes lives today.

CONTENTS

Dedication iii

Acknowledgment iv

About the Author viii

INTRODUCTION x

Week 1: A New Thing Begins 1

Week 2: Strength in the Waiting......................................4

Week 3: The God Who Sees 7

Week 4: God's Faithfulness in Every Season 10

Week 5: Unashamed 13

Week 6: God's Love Letter..16

Week 7: God's Grace in Our Everyday Lives 19

Week 8: Trusting God's Direction...................................22

Week 9: Resting in God's Provision................................25

Week 10: Walking in Forgiveness 28

Week 11: Looking Higher, Not Working Harder 31

Week 12: Hold On to Your Plow......................................34

Week 13: The Strength of Quiet Faith 37

Week 14: Hope in the Waiting...40

Week 15: Bless the Lord, O My Soul 43

Week 16: A Light That Cannot Be Hidden......................46

Week 17: Welcoming the True King 49

Week 18: He Is Risen, Hope Lives 52

Week 19: The Road to Emmaus...55

Week 20: Breakfast with Jesus 58

Week 21: He Believes in You...61

Week 22: Living in Resurrection Hope 64

Week 23: The Lord Is My Shepherd..67

Week 24: God's Healing Touch..70

Week 25: Abiding in the True Vine..73

Week 26: Spirit's Call to Witness..76

Week 27: Living Water and Thirsting for God...............................79

Week 28: Strength in Stillness 82

Week 29: Faith Over Fear..85

Week 30: When God's "Never" Is Always.....................................88

Week 31: The Power of Gentle Words 91

Week 32: Doing the Right Thing, Even When Others Are Not 94

Week 33: Seeds of Kindness...97

Week 34: Seeing Beyond the Giant 100

Week 35: The Door May Not Be Closed 103

Week 36: When a Tree Falls — Living in the Direction You Lean
....106

Week 37: Only the Guilty Need Grace 109

Week 38: The Promiscuous Grace of God 112

Week 39: Remember Whose You Are 115

Week 40: The New Man 118

Week 41: Freedom in Forgiveness 121

Week 42: In Everything, Give Thanks 124

Week 43: The Power of God's Promises 127

Week 44: The Gift of Listening 130

Week 45: Living a Thankful Heart 133

Week 46: Hope That Lasts 136

Week 47: Peace in the Storm 139

Week 48: Joy in the Journey 142

Week 49: Living Like You're Loved 145

Week 50: The Gift of Christ 148

Week 51: Faithful Through Every Season 151

Week 52: Anchored in His Promise 154

Series Conclusion: Walking Forward in Faith 157

About the Author

Pastor Scot is a compassionate shepherd and devoted teacher of God's Word, known for his down-to-earth approach and heart for people from every walk of life. A husband, father, and community leader, Scot has spent years sharing the message of Jesus' love and reconciliation through both word and action.

Rooted in a strong biblical foundation and guided by the Holy Spirit, Scot's ministry reaches beyond the pulpit—extending to the streets, shelters, and communities where hope is most needed. Together with his wife, he leads outreach efforts that provide food, clothing, and the Gospel to those who are often overlooked or forgotten.

His writings blend timeless truth with personal reflection, offering encouragement to believers and an invitation to seekers. Whether speaking to a congregation, teaching in a small group, or writing a devotional, Scot's heart remains the same: to point people to Jesus—the One who saves, heals, and restores.

Scot Saul loves helping people meet God in simple, honest moments. Pastor Scot Saul lives in Prince George, British Columbia and has been in Ministry for well over 20 years.

Page Blank Intentionally

INTRODUCTION

You do not need a perfect day or a perfect track record to meet with God. You only need a few quiet minutes and an honest heart. This book was written to make that meeting simple, steady, and real.

Over time I kept hearing the same things from people who love God and from people who are not sure what they believe. "I am tired." "I am busy." "I want to read the Bible, but I do not know where to start." "I need something clear, kind, and true." This book is my answer to that ache. It is a year of short weekly devotions that meet you where you live, then walk with you one step closer to Jesus.

These pages are not about pressure. They are about presence. Each week follows the same rhythm so you always know what to expect and how to begin.

- **Title** sets the theme for the week.

- **Introduction** names what real life feels like right now.

- **Scripture** gives you God's words before you hear mine.

- **Message** offers a clear, pastor-like reflection that stays rooted in the verse.

- **Encouragement** gives you one or two sentences to carry through the day.

- **Reflection** helps you make it personal with a simple prompt.

- **Notes** gives you space to write, to pray in your own words, or to track what you are sensing.

- **Prayer** closes the time and points you back to God.

The readings are brief on purpose, long enough to be meaningful and short enough to fit inside a real week. The language stays simple, even when the truth is deep. If you are new to the Bible, you will not get lost. If you have walked with Jesus for years, you will still be fed.

Here are a few ways to use this book.

- Pick a regular time each week. Morning is ideal for many, but lunch or evening works as well.

- Read the **Scripture** slowly. Read it out loud if you can.

- Sit with the **Message** and underline what stands out.

- Speak the **Encouragement** to yourself. Let it set the tone for the day.

- Answer the **Reflection** with one honest sentence. You are not writing an essay. You are opening a door.

- Use the **Notes** space freely. Pray in writing, list names, sketch a next step, or record a small grace you noticed.

- Pray the closing **Prayer** in your own voice. Add your own words as needed.

You do not have to move in order. You can begin with the week that matches your need today. Come back to a reading as often as you like. Share a page with a friend. Read with a spouse or a small group. The goal is not to finish a book, the goal is to keep company with Jesus.

If you have felt alone, these pages will remind you that you are seen. If you have felt stuck, they will offer a small next step. If you have felt dry, they will point you to the Living Water. The promise under it all is simple. God is faithful. He knows your name. He meets you in ordinary rooms and walks with you through every season.

I am praying that this book becomes a quiet place where your heart learns to rest, where Scripture becomes familiar and alive, and where hope takes root again. One week at a time, one prayer at a time, one small act of trust at a time, may you discover that God is closer than you thought, kinder than you feared, and strong enough for everything ahead.

Week 1:
A New Thing Begins

Introduction:

A new year, a new season, a new opportunity. Life often feels like we must wait for the perfect moment to begin again, but God offers fresh starts in every season. This devotional will help you recognize His continual work in your life and inspire you to embrace the new beginnings He places before you. Our prayer is that these reflections encourage hope, spark joy, and remind you that God is faithful in every step of the journey.

Scripture:

Isaiah 43:19— "See, I am doing a new thing! Now it springs up; do you not perceive it? I am making a way in the wilderness and streams in the wasteland."

Message:

Every January carries the fragrance of possibility. Calendars reset, habits reboot, and our hearts reach for a cleaner page. Yet Isaiah 43:19 reminds us that God's newness is not limited to the flip of a calendar; it is the steady rhythm of His redemptive heart. Spoken to a people wearied by exile, God's words refused to let the past define the future. He did not dismiss history; He reframed it by His mercy. "Do you not perceive it?" is less a reprimand and more an invitation: lift your eyes to what grace is quietly growing.

Notice the geography of the promise: wilderness and wasteland. God does not wait for ideal conditions to begin His work; He makes

1

a way where there is none and draws water from places that seem incapable of life. This is the gospel pattern: Jesus brings life out of death, beauty out of ashes, and hope out of despair. Our deserts become classrooms of dependence where His love, not our strength, sustains us. We long for God to remove difficulty, yet He often reveals Himself by providing in it: daily bread, unexpected help, a renewed purpose.

Perceiving the "new thing" requires more than optimism; it requires faith anchored in God's character. His grace rewrites what guilt tries to underline. His mercy loosens our grip on failures we cannot fix. His steadfast love nudges us forward when fear prefers familiarity. Sometimes His newness arrives loudly with breakthroughs, reconciliation, and open doors. Often it comes softly with consistent strength for one more step, a fresh hunger for Scripture, and a gentle courage to forgive.

So begin this year not by striving to manufacture change, but by attending to the change God is already initiating. Ask Him to awaken your spiritual senses. Lay yesterday's regrets at the cross and receive the freedom Christ secured. Then take the next faithful step, trusting that streams will meet you in the desert. With that in mind, let us turn our hearts to notice where His newness is already springing up.

Encouragement:

God is already at work. Trust Him to bring beauty from barren places.

Reflection:

Where have you recently felt "wilderness," and how might God be making a quiet way there? Name one sign of His renewing work and one step of faith you will take this week because you believe He is doing a new thing.

Notes:

_____

_____

_____

_____

Keep going. God's newness is nearer than it feels and stronger than what opposes it.

Prayer:

Father, thank You for always doing something new in and around me. Tune my heart to perceive Your hand, loosen my hold on what no longer serves Your purpose, and lead me into the fresh path You are making. By Your grace, give me courage to take the next faithful step and joy to walk it with You. In Jesus' name, amen.

Week 2:
Strength in the Waiting

Introduction:

Waiting is rarely comfortable, yet it is often where growth, faith, and resilience are cultivated. God's timing is perfect, and His faithfulness is steady even when the answer seems delayed. This devotional invites you to pause, reflect, and discover the strength God provides during seasons of waiting, helping you trust Him more fully in the process.

Scripture:

Psalm 27:14— "Wait for the Lord; be strong and take heart and wait for the Lord."

Message:

Waiting can feel like standing still while life rushes past, yet Scripture frames waiting as an active posture of faith. Psalm 27 is David's honest song in the tension between bold trust and real threats. He has enemies, fears, and unanswered questions, and he also has a history with God. That history reorients his present. He does not deny the delay; he submits it to the Lord who has proven faithful. "Wait for the Lord" is not a call to resignation; it is a summons to attention, to watchfulness, prayer, and obedience in the meantime.

Biblically, waiting is tethered to who God is. We wait on the Lord because He is good, sovereign, and timely. His delays are never careless; they are purposeful pauses that form us. Like a seed beneath the soil, unseen work is occurring: roots deepen, resilience strengthens, discernment sharpens. God uses waiting to detach us from outcomes that would define us and to attach us to Himself, the One who sustains us. In this way, waiting becomes worship: choosing trust over control, and Presence over panic.

Notice the double charge: "be strong and take heart." Strength here is not bravado; it is grace-fueled perseverance. To "take heart" is to let courage rise from God's promises rather than from visible progress. You may not be able to speed the process, but you can steward the pause: keep praying when feelings cool, keep obeying when clarity lags, keep serving when doors seem shut. God is not idle in your waiting. He is aligning circumstances, preparing people, and shaping you to carry what you have asked Him for.

When we look back, we often see that the waiting room was the workshop: character forged, motives purified, hope anchored not in the gift but in the Giver. If you are in that room now, lift your eyes. The Lord you are waiting for is also the Lord who is with you. With that assurance, turn your attention to where His quiet work may already be unfolding.

Encouragement:

Your waiting is not wasted. He is shaping strength and hope beneath the surface.

Reflection:

Where is God inviting you to "be strong and take heart" today, and what one area will you entrust to Him without trying to control the timing? Name one faithful step you will take this week as an act of trust while you wait.

Notes:

_____

_____

_____

_____

Hold fast. God's timing is kind, and His Presence is your strength.

Prayer:

Lord, I admit that waiting stretches me. Yet I choose to trust Your heart and Your timing. Steady my steps, strengthen my faith, and teach me to worship while I wait. Help me to act in obedience today and to rest in Your faithful care. In Jesus' name, amen.

Week 3:
The God Who Sees

Introduction:

Life can often leave us feeling overlooked, misunderstood, or unseen. In those moments, it is easy to question whether anyone truly notices the struggles we endure or the quiet acts of faith we carry in our hearts. This devotional reminds us that God sees us fully, intimately, and with unwavering compassion. As you read, may you be encouraged to trust that nothing escapes His notice, and that His Presence is constant even in the wilderness moments of life. We pray these reflections bring comfort, hope, and a renewed awareness of God's attentive love for you.

Scripture:

Genesis 16:13— "She gave this name to the Lord who spoke to her: 'You are the God who sees me,' for she said, 'I have now seen the One who sees me.'"

Message:

Hagar's story unfolds at the painful intersection of powerlessness and rejection. A servant caught in a broken household dynamic, she runs into the desert with nothing but fear and fatigue. It is precisely there, away from the places where people should have cared, that the Lord meets her. He calls her by name, asks after her heart, and gives wise direction for her steps. Hagar responds with a confession that has comforted weary souls for centuries: "El Roi" - the God who sees me.

God's seeing is not cold surveillance; it is warm, personal, and

7

purposeful. He does not merely observe our circumstances; He interprets them through His compassion and covenant. The angel of the Lord does not minimize Hagar's pain, yet He reframes her future with promise: God hears, God will provide, God will write a story beyond this moment. Scripture echoes this theme. The Lord numbers our hairs, keeps our tears in a bottle, and watches not to accuse but to care. His gaze carries mercy.

In Christ, this compassionate seeing draws even nearer. Jesus embodies God's attentive heart. He looks upon crowds with compassion, notices the overlooked widow, calls Zacchaeus by name, and restores the outcast with dignity. On the cross, the God who sees also suffers for the seen, proving that His knowledge of us is not detached information but sacrificial love. Because of Jesus, we are not named by our wounds but by His work: beloved, redeemed, chosen.

Practically, being seen by God anchors our worth beyond public recognition. Our culture assigns value by visibility: platforms, metrics, and applause. The kingdom assigns value by Presence: "The Lord knows those who are His." This frees us to practice uncelebrated faithfulness, praying in secret, serving without fanfare, and persevering when no one else notices, confident that our Father, who sees in secret, rewards with Himself.

How do we live into this truth? Learn the rhythm of naming and noticing. Name where you feel unseen and bring it honestly to the Lord who calls you by name. Then notice where His care has already met you: small provisions, timely words, quiet strength. A simple daily examen, asking "Where did I sense Your attentive love today, and where did I forget it?" can retrain the heart to live under His kind gaze.

When loneliness whispers, "You are invisible," answer with Hagar's testimony: "I have seen the One who sees me." Let that truth settle your heart and steady your hope. With that assurance in place, pause and listen for where His attentive love is meeting you today.

Encouragement:

You are never invisible to God. He sees, knows, and loves you deeply.

Reflection:

Where do you most need the reminder that God sees you, and what response of faith will you take this week because His compassionate gaze defines your story rather than your circumstances?

Notes:

_____

_____

_____

_____

Take heart. His eyes are on you, and His love will not look away.

Prayer:

Lord, thank You that You are the God who sees. When I feel alone or overlooked, remind me that Your eyes are kind and constant. Call me by name, steady my steps, and help me rest in Your watchful care. In Jesus' name, amen.

Week 4:

God's Faithfulness in Every Season

Introduction:

Every season of life carries its own challenges and joys, and sometimes it is easy to feel unsteady when circumstances shift around us. Yet God's faithfulness remains constant, a steady anchor amid change and uncertainty. This devotional invites you to reflect on His unwavering love, His daily mercies, and the assurance that He walks with you in every season. May these reflections encourage your heart and strengthen your trust in His steadfast Presence.

Scripture:

Lamentations 3:22-23— "Because of the Lord's great love, we are not consumed, for his compassions never fail. They are new every morning; great is your faithfulness."

Message:

Lamentations is a book of tears, yet in the very center of its sorrow rises a hymn of hope. Jerusalem lies in ruins, Jeremiah's heart is broken, and grief seems to have the last word. But the prophet lifts his eyes above the rubble and remembers what pain can never cancel: the steadfast love of the Lord. The Hebrew word behind "great love" is *hesed*, God's covenant kindness, loyal love that refuses to let go. "Compassions" translates *rachamim*, tender mercies that flow from a heart moved with affection. Together they announce that we are held, not consumed.

Notice the cadence: "new every morning." God's mercy is not stale leftovers from yesterday; it is a fresh provision matched to today's needs. Like manna in the wilderness, His compassion meets us in daily portions, sufficient for sorrow, strong for temptation, and gentle for weariness. We often want a year's worth of answers at once, but our Father trains our hearts to trust Him a day at a time.

God's faithfulness is not fragile, and it is not dependent on our feelings. It is rooted in His unchanging character and revealed supremely in Christ. At the cross, love did not fail us; it rescued us. In the resurrection, mercy did not run out; it overflowed into new life. Because Jesus lives, every morning arrives under a banner that reads, "Great is Your faithfulness."

How do we live this in shifting seasons? First, remember: rehearse the ways God has carried you. Journal, testify, and pray Scripture back to Him. Second, receive: open your hands to the mercy appointed for this day. Do not borrow tomorrow's anxieties. Third, respond: faithfulness begets faithfulness. Practice small obediences, keep showing up, and bless others with the comfort you have received. When autumns of loss turn to winters of waiting, His love remains. When springs of renewal bloom into summers of abundance, His love remains. The seasons change, but the Anchor holds.

With that anchor in place, name where His fresh mercies are meeting you right now and where you need them most.

Encouragement:

God's faithfulness is your steady foundation. Trust Him through every season.

Reflection:

Where have you seen God's "new every morning" mercy recently, and where do you need to trust His faithfulness today? Identify one simple act of trust you will practice this week.

Notes:

_____

_____

_____

_____

Take courage. Tomorrow's mercies will be there when tomorrow comes.

Prayer:

Lord, thank You that Your *hesed* never fails and Your mercies rise with every dawn. In seasons of loss and seasons of laughter, teach me to remember Your goodness, receive today's grace, and respond in faithful obedience. Steady my heart when I feel unmoored, and anchor me again in Your unchanging love. In Jesus' name, amen.

Week 5:

Unashamed

Introduction:

In a world that pressures us to conform or hide our true selves, God calls us to live boldly in His truth. This devotional invites you to embrace your identity in Christ, to step forward unashamed, and to experience the freedom and confidence that comes from being fully known and fully loved by Him.

Scripture:

Romans 1:16— "For I am not ashamed of the gospel, because it is the power of God that brings salvation to everyone who believes…"

Message:

Paul writes to believers in Rome, the cultural center of power and reputation, and declares, "I am not ashamed of the gospel." Why such boldness? Because the gospel is not a hobby or an opinion; it is the power of God that rescues, reconciles, and renews. The message we carry does not rest on our eloquence but on God's action in Christ: Jesus crucified for our sins, raised in glory, and reigning as Lord. What the world may call foolish or naive (see 1 Corinthians 1:18) is, in fact, the wisdom and strength of God.

Shame thrives where identity is uncertain. The gospel answers with a new name and a new belonging. In Christ you are chosen and brought out of darkness into marvelous light (1 Peter 2:9). You are not propping up a passing ideology; you are standing inside God's eternal story of grace. This is why Paul can be unashamed. His confidence is rooted not in himself but in the faithfulness of God, who saves "everyone who believes," breaking every barrier of background, status, or story.

We know the subtle pressures: keep faith private, smooth the rough edges of truth, avoid the name of Jesus. But love does not hide what heals. To be unashamed is not to be unkind; it is to speak truth with humility, to hold convictions with gentleness, and to embody grace under pressure. The same Spirit that raised Jesus empowers us to witness (Acts 1:8) with integrity: doing our work honestly, forgiving when wronged, serving those in need, and explaining the hope within us with gentleness and respect.

Living unashamed means letting Christ shape both our words and our ways. In conversations, resist cynicism and offer hope. In decisions, choose obedience over convenience. In suffering, endure with joy because your Savior endured for you. None of this is performance; it is participation in the life of the One who loved you first. When fear whispers, "Be quiet," grace answers, "Be faithful." With that confidence, name where He is inviting you to bold and loving witness today.

Encouragement:

Do not apologize for the light within you. Walk with confidence, speak with love, and live joyfully in the truth of the gospel.

Reflection:

Where are you most tempted to hide your faith, and how will you take a courageous, loving step to honor Christ this week?

Notes:

_____

_____

_____

_____

Lift your head. Christ in you is strong, kind, and more than enough.

Prayer:

Lord, give me the courage to live unashamed of You. May my life reflect Your love, and may I speak truth with humility and grace. Strengthen me to stand for what is right and to remember the power of the gospel. In Jesus' name, amen.

Week 6:

God's Love Letter

Introduction:

Love is more than a feeling. It is the heartbeat of God's relationship with us. This devotional reflects on God's personal, unwavering love for you. As we explore His Word and heart, may you be reminded that you are cherished, pursued, and held in His care every day.

Scripture:

Romans 5:8— "But God demonstrates his own love for us in this: While we were still sinners, Christ died for us."

Message:

Paul does not define God's love with vague sentiment; he anchors it in a public act of history: Christ crucified. "God demonstrates his own love," not merely declares it, by giving His Son when we were neither neutral nor deserving, but still sinners. The gospel does not meet us at our best; it moves toward us at our worst. This is love revealed, not guessed at; proven, not presumed.

Consider the direction of this love. It is not love we climbed up to, but love that descended to us. Before we could tidy our stories or repair our failures, Christ bore our sin, absorbed our shame, and opened the way back to the Father. Grace is not God lowering His standards; it is God lifting us by the finished work of Jesus to stand righteous in Him. The cross shows that God's love is holy, dealing truthfully with sin, and merciful, covering sinners with pardon. Justice and love do not compete at Calvary; they embrace.

Scripture calls this love everlasting and drawing: "I have loved you with an everlasting love; I have drawn you with unfailing kindness" (Jeremiah 31:3). God's love is both root and river, rooted in His unchanging character and a river that keeps pursuing our weary hearts. When doubts speak, the cross replies. When accusations rise, the blood of Jesus answers. When loneliness lingers, the Spirit pours God's love into our hearts. We are not loved because we are lovely; we become lovely because we are loved.

What changes when this love is received? Identity shifts from performer to beloved. Wounds begin to heal under the warmth of divine kindness. The forgiven become forgiving; the welcomed become welcoming; those carried by grace become carriers of grace. This is not theory; it is a daily reality to be practiced: confessing sin quickly because love is safe, praying boldly because love invites, serving joyfully because love overflows.

So read God's "love letter" not as a general memo to humanity but as a personal word with your name on it. At the cross, Love signed in crimson, "For you." With that assurance, notice how His love is reshaping your life today.

Encouragement:

God's love is your unshakable foundation. Receive it, and let it flow through you.

Reflection:

How does God's unconditional love reshape how you see yourself and others, and what is one practical way you will reflect His kindness in a relationship this week?

Notes:

_____

_____

_____

_____

Rest easy. God's love reached you first and will not let you go.

Prayer:

Lord, thank You for loving me in my brokenness and calling me Your own. Help me grasp the height, depth, and breadth of Your love. Teach me to live from acceptance, not for it, to forgive as I have been forgiven, and to serve with grace. Let Your love renew my mind and steady my steps today. In Jesus' name, amen.

Week 7:

God's Grace in Our Everyday Lives

Introduction:

Grace is not just a theological concept; it is the lifeline that sustains us daily. This devotional encourages you to see God's unmerited favor at work in the ordinary moments of life, offering strength, patience, and peace. Our prayer is that these reflections help you rest in His grace and recognize His ongoing Presence.

Scripture:

Ephesians 2:8–9— "For it is by grace you have been saved, through faith, and this is not from yourselves, it is the gift of God, not by works, so that no one can boast."

Message:

Paul's words in Ephesians draw a bright line through our spiritual lives: salvation is by grace, through faith, not from ourselves. Grace is not God's polite nod to our efforts; it is His decisive rescue for the helpless. We bring empty hands; He brings everything. The same grace that saves also sustains. It is not a doorway we step through once, but a home we live in daily.

Think of grace in three textures. First, justifying grace: God declares us righteous in Christ. Our status before Him is settled, not fluctuating with our performance. On our best days we cannot add to it, and on our worst days, we cannot subtract from it. Second, sanctifying grace: the Spirit trains us to say no to sin and yes to holiness (Titus 2:11–12). Grace is not moral leniency; it is transforming power, desire and ability to live as beloved children. Third, sustaining grace: in weakness, God says, "My grace is sufficient… my power is made perfect in weakness" (2 Corinthians 12:9). Where our strength ends, His begins.

How does this look in ordinary life? Grace steadies a hurried morning with the reminder that we are loved before we lift a finger. Grace calms an anxious heart in a hard meeting and gives patience when conversation frays. Grace meets us after failure, not with condemnation, but with correction and courage to try again. Grace also reshapes success, guarding us from pride by whispering that this, too, is a gift. Even our hunger for God is energized by grace, drawing us back to Scripture and prayer when we would rather numb out.

We do not graduate from grace; we grow in it. Practically, that means coming again and again to the throne of grace to receive mercy and help (Hebrews 4:16). It means preaching the gospel to our own souls: I am saved by grace, upheld by grace, and sent by grace. It means exchanging self-reliance for Spirit-reliance in the small, unseen places: apologizing quickly, forgiving freely, serving quietly, trusting deeply. Grace is the music under all our days. Listen closely and you will hear it, stronger than your striving and kinder than your fears.

Encouragement:

God's grace is always sufficient. Lean into His love each day, whatever the season holds.

Reflection:

Where have you experienced God's everyday grace recently, and how will you respond with gratitude and trust in one ordinary moment this week?

Notes:

_____

_____

_____

_____

Take heart. Grace met you today and will meet you again tomorrow.

Prayer:

Lord, thank You for Your incredible grace that meets me where I am. Teach me to rely on Your strength, not my own, to receive correction without shame and mercy without doubt. Let Your grace shape my thoughts, words, and choices today. In Jesus' name, amen.

Week 8:

Trusting God's Direction

Introduction:

Life often feels unpredictable, and even our best-laid plans can take unexpected turns. In these moments, we remember that God's wisdom surpasses our understanding and His guidance is steadfast. This devotional invites you to explore what it means to truly trust God, not only when it is easy, but especially when the way seems unclear. May these reflections encourage you to release your need for certainty and step confidently into the paths He is preparing for you, knowing that He sees, knows, and leads every step of your journey.

Scripture:

Proverbs 3:5–6—"Trust in the Lord with all your heart and lean not on your own understanding; in all your ways submit to him, and he will make your paths straight."

Message:

Life rarely moves in a straight line. Plans change, doors close, and detours appear without explanation. Proverbs 3:5–6 does not promise a path without bends; it promises a God who walks with you at every turn. Trusting the Lord with all your heart is more than agreeing that He is reliable. It is transferring the weight of your life, your hopes and timelines, your fears and what-ifs, onto His unshakable character. You are not asked to ignore wisdom or deny reality; you are invited to stop enthroning your limited perspective as the final authority. Your understanding is a useful guide, but it is not a worthy god.

To submit your ways to Him is deeply relational. The word "acknowledge" pictures a daily companionship: pausing to pray before you plan, letting His Word define what straight actually means, welcoming wise counsel when your view narrows, and slowing your pace enough to hear His quiet leading. In that posture, obedience becomes the doorway to clarity. God often straightens the path as you move, not before you move. The next faithful step rarely arrives with fireworks; it comes as a settled nudge aligned with Scripture and confirmed over time by peace and perseverance.

Straight does not always mean simple. It means aligned, your steps tuned to His wisdom, and your desires gradually harmonized with His will. Even in fog, the Shepherd knows the terrain. He is not asking you to manufacture courage; He is imparting it as you lean. When anxiety rises, entrust the unknown to the One who knows you fully. When impatience urges shortcuts, remember that shortcuts often detour character, while God's timing matures it. When fear tells you to retreat, recall that the safest place is not the most predictable plan, but the most obedient posture.

Lift your eyes. You do not need the entire map to move forward today. Ask the Lord what faithfulness looks like in this hour, take that step, and let tomorrow's turn be tomorrow's grace. As you walk, expect the quiet miracles of guidance: doors you could not open easing wide, paths you could not see becoming clear, and a growing confidence that the One who leads you is also the One who keeps you.

Encouragement:

You do not have to see the whole path. God's direction is trustworthy and sure.

Reflection:

Where have you been leaning on your own understanding, and what single step of obedience will you take this week to entrust that area to God's leading?

Notes:

_____

_____

_____

_____

Keep walking. The One who leads you also walks beside you.

Prayer:

Father, help me to trust You more fully. Where I have relied on my own understanding, teach me to lean on You. Guide my steps, align my heart with Your wisdom, and give me peace as I follow Your lead. In Jesus' name, amen.

Week 9:

Resting in God's Provision

Introduction:

Life can feel heavy with responsibilities, uncertainties, and the pressure to provide for ourselves and others. Yet God's invitation is simple: to trust Him and rest in His faithful provision. This devotional will guide you to pause and consider how His care extends beyond material needs into the peace, strength, and wisdom that sustain you daily. May these reflections help you release worry, fix your eyes on His kingdom, and embrace the confidence that He sees, knows, and provides for every part of your life.

Scripture:

Matthew 6:31–33— "So do not worry, saying, 'What shall we eat?' or 'What shall we drink?' or 'What shall we wear?' ... But seek first his kingdom and his righteousness, and all these things will be given to you as well."

Message:

Jesus speaks to our anxious hearts with a gentle but decisive command: do not worry. His words in the Sermon on the Mount do not dismiss real needs; they relocate them beneath a greater reality, our Father's care. The invitation is not to passivity but to priority. We still plan, budget, labor, and steward; we simply refuse to enthrone anxiety as our master. To seek first is to set the compass of the heart toward God's reign, trusting that provision aligns itself to a kingdom-directed life.

Consider the birds and lilies Jesus points to. They neither hoard nor hurry, yet the Father feeds and clothes them with a splendor beyond Solomon. Creation itself becomes a sermon: you are seen, valued, and kept. Worry promises control but delivers exhaustion. Faith surrenders control and discovers rest. When we loosen our grip on outcomes and tighten our hold on God's character, we find that provision is not only bread on the table but peace in the soul. Sometimes God supplies by opening doors. Sometimes by closing them to protect us. Sometimes by giving daily manna, just enough for today, with the promise of fresh mercies tomorrow.

Scripture widens the lens: "My God will meet all your needs according to the riches of his glory in Christ Jesus" (Philippians 4:19). Needs, not greeds. According to His riches, not our limits. Provision may arrive as strength to endure, wisdom for a complex choice, a timely word from a friend, or the courage to ask for help. It may be a new job, or it may be contentment that quiets the craving for a different life. In every case, the cross assures us that our greatest need, reconciliation with God, has already been met so that lesser needs can be entrusted to His faithful hand.

Think back on your own story. How many just-in-time graces appeared when you had no margin left? How often did peace come when the situation had not changed, but you had? Let those memories teach your heart to release the fear of tomorrow and receive today's portion with gratitude. With that posture of trust, turn toward the places where He is inviting you to rest in His care now.

Encouragement:

God sees your needs, even the unspoken ones, and He is faithful to provide.

Reflection:

Where do you need to trust more deeply in God's provision, whether material, emotional, or spiritual, and what practical choice will you make this week to rest in His care there?

Notes:

_____

_____

_____

_____

Breathe easy. Tomorrow's grace will meet tomorrow's need, and today you are held.

Prayer:

Father, thank You for being my Provider. I confess the ways worry has ruled my thoughts. Reorder my priorities around Your kingdom, calm my heart with Your peace, and teach me to work diligently while resting confidently in Your care. Meet my needs according to Your riches in Christ Jesus. Amen.

Week 10:

Walking in Forgiveness

Introduction:

Forgiveness is rarely easy, yet it is essential for peace and freedom. This devotional invites you to pause and reflect on God's call to extend grace to others, just as He has lavished His forgiveness upon you. Consider how releasing resentment can lighten your heart, mend relationships, and allow God's healing Presence to flow through your life.

Scripture:

Ephesians 4:32— "Be kind and compassionate to one another, forgiving each other, just as in Christ God forgave you."

Message:

Forgiveness sits at the very center of the gospel. Paul does not ground the command in our willpower but in God's prior action: forgiving each other just as in Christ God forgave you. The cross is the measure and the motive. God did not wait for us to become worthy or even willing. While we were still sinners, Christ died for us. When we survey that grace, our reasons for withholding forgiveness begin to loosen. We are not asked to minimize wrong or ignore wounds. We are invited to bring them to the place where justice and mercy met, Calvary, and let Christ's finished work reshape our response.

In a season of confession and turning, we remember that we stand where every forgiven person stands: at the foot of the cross, empty-handed and fully loved. From that ground, forgiveness becomes more than a moral duty. It becomes a Spirit-enabled participation in Jesus' life. Colossians echoes the call to bear with each other and forgive. Bearing with does not deny pain; it carries it to God and refuses to pass it along. Forgiveness is both an event and a process. Sometimes it is a decisive moment; often it is a daily choosing. The feelings may lag, but obedience can lead, and grace can heal what time alone cannot.

To forgive is not to excuse harm or abandon wisdom. Boundaries can be a faithful expression of love, and reconciliation, when possible, requires truth, repentance, and rebuilding trust. Yet the first movement is inward: we release the right to revenge and entrust justice to the Lord who judges rightly. In doing so, we step out from under bitterness, which corrodes the soul and silences joy. Forgiveness frees us to pray blessings where we once rehearsed injury, to speak truth without poison, and to look forward without being chained to the past.

If you struggle, begin where Jesus teaches, by remembering how much you have been forgiven. The parable of the unmerciful servant is not a threat so much as a mirror. Those who drink deeply of mercy are meant to become its conduits. Ask the Spirit to align your heart with the prayer you whisper, "Forgive us our debts, as we also have forgiven our debtors," and then take one step: write a note, release a debt, stop rehearsing a grievance, bless an enemy by name. The One who commands also supplies; His grace meets your weakness with power to love.

Encouragement:

God's forgiveness empowers you to forgive. His grace will meet you in every step toward freedom.

Reflection:

Where is the Lord inviting you to extend forgiveness, and what specific grace-filled action will you take this week to begin walking in that freedom?

Notes:

_____

_____

_____

_____

Take heart. Mercy has already made the first move, and it will carry you the rest of the way.

Prayer:

Lord, thank You for forgiving me through Jesus. I bring you the hurts I carry and the anger I too easily nurse. Soften my heart, steady my voice with truth and compassion, and teach me to release debts as You have released mine. Lead me in the freedom of Your peace. Amen.

Week 11:

Looking Higher, Not Working Harder

Introduction:

In a world that praises busyness and productivity, we can easily grow weary from the push to do more and prove ourselves. This week's devotional invites you to pause and choose a different way, the way of rest and trust in Jesus. As we hear His invitation to take His yoke upon us, may you lift your eyes, release the weight of striving, and embrace the peace that comes from walking in step with Him.

Scripture:

Matthew 11:28–30— "Come to me, all you who are weary and burdened, and I will give you rest. Take my yoke upon you and learn from me, for I am gentle and humble in heart, and you will find rest for your souls. For my yoke is easy and my burden is light."

Message:

Jesus does not offer a technique for rest. He offers Himself. "Come to me" is the doorway to the soul-rest we try to manufacture with tighter schedules and harder effort. An inner taskmaster often mutters, You're behind, do more, be more. Even our spiritual lives can bend toward performance until the means replace the Master. Jesus interrupts that cycle with a new rhythm: not achieve but abide, not try harder but draw nearer.

His image of the yoke is tender and wise. A yoke joins two to walk together. In the fields, a strong, seasoned animal is yoked with a younger one so the experienced pace sets the stride, carries the weight, and trains without breaking. When you take Jesus' yoke, you are not handed another burden. You are joined to a Person whose gentleness sets your pace and whose strength bears what you cannot. He promises not a momentary breather but rest for your soul. That is rest beneath the work: a settled assurance that you are loved, led, and held while you labor.

Learning from Him revises our definitions. Rest is not the absence of responsibility. It is the Presence of Christ in responsibility. Obedience remains, but the engine changes from anxiety to grace. You can plan without panic because He carries tomorrow. You can serve without posturing because He secures your worth. You can say no without guilt because His yoke fits your frame. Lay down the yoke of self-reliance and receive the yoke of Jesus—lighter not because life is easy, but because love carries the weight.

Pause and lift your eyes. Confess the hurry that has shaped your habits and the pressure that has narrowed your prayers. Choose again to match your stride to His, and let His gentle heart set your pace.

Encouragement:

Jesus never asked you to carry it all. His gentle heart sets the pace and shares the load.

Reflection:

Where are you feeling pressure to perform or prove yourself, and what specific burden will you lay down as you turn your gaze to Jesus and receive His rest this week?

Notes:

_____

_____

_____

_____

Lift your eyes. His yoke fits, His heart is kind, and His rest is real.

Prayer:

Lord, I come to You weary from striving. Teach me your pace. Replace my self-reliance with Your grace, my hurry with Your Presence, and my fear with Your peace. I take Your yoke today. Lead me and give rest to my soul. Amen.

Week 12:

Hold On to Your Plow

Introduction:

There are moments when following Jesus feels exhilarating and others when it feels costly. Temptations to look back, slow down, or second-guess can tug at our resolve. Christ calls us to a steady, forward gaze. Discipleship is not part-time. It is a whole-life yes.

Scripture:

Luke 9:62— "Jesus replied, 'No one who puts a hand to the plow and looks back is fit for service in the kingdom of God.'"

Message:

Jesus spoke these words on the road as would-be followers offered half-yeses padded with conditions. The image He chose is earthy and clear: a hand gripping a plow. In ancient fields, a farmer fixed their eyes on a mark ahead to keep the furrow straight. One backward glance and the line veered. Jesus is not scolding hesitation for its own sake. He is exposing the divided heart that tries to follow Him while courting old allegiances.

We feel that pull to look back. What if I miss the life I left? What if obedience costs too much? Yet the kingdom advances through undivided devotion. When you grip the plow, you are not volunteering for a sprint. You are choosing a long obedience that produces a harvest in due time. The forward mark is not your comfort or plan. It is Christ Himself, the Author and Perfecter of faith.

Elisha gives a living picture. When Elijah called him, Elisha burned his plow and sacrificed his oxen, feasting the village before stepping into prophetic service. He did not keep the equipment "just in case" (1 Kings 19:19–21). That bonfire was a declaration: no return route, no split loyalty. You may not burn farm tools, but you can surrender exit ramps, habits that dilute your witness, narratives that keep you small, comforts that compete for first love.

Holding the plow does not mean you never stumble. It means when weariness whispers, you tighten your grip. When nostalgia paints Egypt in soft colors, you remember the chains. When fear threatens your stride, you fix your eyes again on Jesus. He is not a distant taskmaster. He is the Lord who walks the rows with you, and He has already borne the cost of your faltering. Grace does not loosen your hold. It strengthens it. With every faithful pass down the field, prayer whispered, kindness offered, truth spoken, temptation resisted, the furrow of your life straightens toward harvest. And that harvest belongs to God.

Encouragement:

You are not plowing alone. Christ is before you, beside you, and within you. Keep your hand steady; a harvest is forming.

Reflection:

What "look back" tug most tempts you to loosen your grip, and what one concrete step will you take this week to keep your eyes fixed on Jesus and say, "No turning back?"

Notes:

_____

_____

_____

_____

Take a moment to listen and write. God's whispers grow clearer when you pause.

Prayer:

Lord Jesus, I place my hand to the plow again. Forgive the backward glances and the divided loves. Set my gaze on You, strengthen my grip by Your grace, and straighten the furrow of my days for Your glory. When I grow weary, remind me that You are faithful and the harvest is Yours. Amen.

Week 13:

The Strength of Quiet Faith

Introduction:

Sometimes life feels loud, chaotic, and demanding. In these moments, faith can seem small or invisible. Yet God often works most powerfully in the quiet, unseen places of trust and obedience. Quiet faith is not passive. It is steadfast, enduring, and deeply rooted in God's promises.

Scripture:

Habakkuk 2:4— "...the righteous person will live by his faithfulness."

Message:

Faith rarely makes headlines. It usually grows in hidden places: before dawn with an open Bible, in a whispered prayer at the sink, in a choice to forgive when no one is watching. Habakkuk's world shook with injustice and delay, and into that confusion God declared that life with Him is sustained not by visible outcomes but by faithful trust. This is not a denial of reality. It is a steady turning toward God when the path is dim and the answers are slow.

Elijah knew the weight of discouragement after Carmel. Fire fell, fear followed, and he fled to a cave convinced he was alone. God did not shout him down. He met him in a whisper. Strength returned in Presence, and Elijah rose to continue the work God still had for him. Daniel's life sings the same tune. He did not wage his battles on public stages first. He opened his windows toward Jerusalem and prayed day after day, quietly faithful. Lions could not devour what a lifetime of trust had formed. Quiet faith is not weakness. It is courage trained over time, obedience repeated until it becomes reflex.

"Be still, and know that I am God," Psalm 46 says. Stillness is not inaction. It is inner surrender that allows God to be God. Quiet faith waits without giving up, works without self-exaltation, and hopes without timelines. It shapes humility and dependence, tuning our ears to God's guidance so we can obey a gentle nudge as readily as a clear command. In a culture that prizes speed and applause, to keep showing up, praying again, serving again, trusting again, is a revolutionary act of worship.

When you cannot see what God is doing, remember who He is. Rehearse His past faithfulness until the present quiet begins to hum with promise. Take the next faithful step, send the note, make the call, open the Word, kneel to pray, trusting that God's hidden work is no less real for being unseen. Quiet seeds become sturdy trees. Quiet faith becomes a strong life.

Encouragement:

Even when no one notices, God does. Your quiet faith delights His heart and shapes your life.

Reflection:

Where is God inviting you to trust Him quietly, without immediate proof or recognition, and what small act of unseen obedience will you take this week to live by faith?

Notes:

Take heart. What you plant in quiet trust, God grows into durable joy.

Prayer:

Lord, teach me to live by faith in the silent and unseen places. Settle my soul in Your promises, tune my ears to Your whisper, and strengthen me to keep obeying when results are slow and applause is absent. I trust Your timing, Your wisdom, and Your faithful love. Amen.

Week 14:
Hope in the Waiting

Introduction:

Waiting is often uncomfortable and frustrating. Scripture shows that waiting is not wasted time. It is a sacred season in which God works unseen, strengthening faith, refining character, and preparing us for what lies ahead.

Scripture:

Isaiah 40:31—"But those who hope in the Lord will renew their strength. They will soar on wings like eagles; they will run and not grow weary, they will walk and not be faint."

Message:

Isaiah's promise does not deny fatigue. It declares where fresh strength is found. "Those who hope in the Lord" speaks of a braided trust. Like strands woven together, your weakness is intertwined with His power. Waiting is not idling in a stalled lane. It is fastening your life to God's steady character. The Lord calls you to an active posture, seeking Him in prayer, listening to His Word, and aligning your pace to His timing.

Scripture is honest about the long arc of God's purposes. Abraham and Sarah waited decades for a child and learned that promise ripens at God's speed. Joseph waited in the shadows of injustice, and the prison that confined him became the platform God used to shape wisdom for a nation. David waited between anointing and the crown and wrote psalms that still steady weary hearts. These seasons were not empty. They were corridors of formation. In waiting, God loosens your grip on outcomes and tightens your hold on Him. You learn to distinguish between what is urgent and what is essential, between your schedule and His sovereignty.

Isaiah's imagery is tender and true. There are days of soaring when grace lifts you beyond what you thought possible. There are stretches of running when endurance is needed and given. There are long, ordinary miles of walking when no fireworks flare and yet you do not faint. The same Lord supplies strength for each pace. Hope does not always look like wings. Sometimes it looks like one more faithful step.

To wait with hope is to practice holy attention. Keep company with God in the meantime. Name disappointments to Him rather than to your fears. Feed your heart with His promises. Notice the small evidences of His care: the needed word at the right time, the courage to choose obedience again, the peace that settles where panic used to live. "Wait for the Lord; be strong and take heart," Psalm 27:14 says. Strength is not summoned from within. It is shared from above. Like an eagle riding thermals, learn to catch the updraft of His Presence rather than flapping in your own effort.

Ask for eyes to see the quiet work of God while the visible answer tarries. Lay your timelines before Him, receive today's grace, and trust that the One who began a good work in you will not leave it unfinished.

Encouragement:

Hope in God sustains and strengthens you now while He prepares blessings you cannot yet see.

Reflection:

What area of your life most needs hope and trust while you wait on God's timing, and how will you braid your weakness to His strength with a specific practice this week?

Notes:

_____

_____

_____

_____

Take heart. While you wait, He works, and His strength is already on the way.

Prayer:

Lord, I place my waiting in Your hands. Renew my strength as I hope in You. Teach me to soar when You lift me, to run when endurance is needed, and to walk without fainting when the path is long. I trust Your timing and Your heart toward me. Amen.

Week 15:

Bless the Lord, O My Soul

Introduction:

There are days when the heart feels light and worship comes easily. There are other days when the soul feels heavy and tired. David knew this tension, yet he did not let emotions decide his worship. He spoke to his own soul and called it to bless the Lord.

Scripture:

Psalm 103:1— "Praise the Lord, my soul; all my inmost being, praise his holy name."

Message:

In Christ, your Spirit is secure and sealed with the Holy Spirit (Ephesians 1:13). Your soul, however, still weathers storms of anxiety, apathy, and ache. That is why Psalm 103 begins with an instruction to oneself. "Praise the Lord, my soul." David does not wait for feelings to lift. He summons his soul to align with truth.

He does this by remembering. He tells his soul not to forget the Lord's benefits, then he names them until gratitude outshouts gloom. The Lord forgives all sin. Shame's verdict is overruled at the cross, and the record against you is cancelled. He heals and restores. Wounds within and without meet a physician who mends what seemed unmendable. He redeems life from the pit. Where despair narrows your horizon, God reaches in and pulls you up. He crowns you with steadfast love and compassion. A bowed head is circled with royal kindness that does not let go. He satisfies with good things so that your youth is renewed like the eagle's. Strength rises where weariness had settled, and hope catches the lift of grace.

To bless the Lord is not to deny pain. It is to declare God's goodness in the middle of it. Habakkuk learned this song when fields were bare and stalls were empty. "Yet I will rejoice in the Lord" (Habakkuk 3:17–18). Circumstances did not preach his praise. God's character did. When your soul is downcast, speak what is eternally true. The Lord is compassionate and gracious, slow to anger and abounding in love. He does not treat us as our sins deserve. His love is from everlasting to everlasting (Psalm 103:8 –17).

This is the practice of holy self-talk. Do not let your soul lead worship. Let worship lead your soul. Open Scripture and rehearse His benefits until remembrance becomes rejoicing. Choose gratitude before you feel it. Choose obedience before you see it. Choose praise before you perceive the outcome. God meets you in the act. As truth takes root, heaviness loosens, and your inmost being rises to bless His holy name.

Encouragement:

Your Spirit is safe in Christ, and your soul can learn to sing again. Start by telling it the truth God has already spoken.

Reflection:

When your soul is downcast, which truth about God do you most need today, and what simple practice will help you remember it each day this week: His forgiveness, His healing, His steadfast love, or His renewing strength?

Notes:

_____

_____

_____

_____

Begin to bless Him. Truth will lead your soul where feelings cannot.

Prayer:

Father, thank You that my salvation is secure in You. When my soul is heavy, teach me to remember Your benefits and to speak Your Word over my life. Form in me a reflex of praise in every season, and let my whole being bless Your holy name. Amen.

Week 16:

A Light That Cannot Be Hidden

Introduction:

Even in the midst of celebration and tradition, God's truth often whispers beneath the surface. This week, we reflect on the power of light and how a life surrendered to Jesus can shine and transform the world nearby. The story of St. Patrick encourages us to let our faith be visible in everyday obedience, courage, and grace.

Scripture:

Matthew 5:14–16 — "You are the light of the world. A town built on a hill cannot be hidden. Neither do people light a lamp and put it under a bowl. Instead, they put it on its stand, and it gives light to everyone in the house. In the same way, let your light shine before others, that they may see your good deeds and glorify your Father in heaven."

Message:

St. Patrick's Day often bursts with parades and seas of green, yet beneath the festivity lies a testimony of grace. Patrick was carried to Ireland as an enslaved teenager. In loneliness, he learned the nearness of Christ. After a daring escape and return to Britain, he could have closed the chapter. Instead, the love of God sent him back, not to reclaim power, but to proclaim redemption. He returned to the place of his suffering with the gospel, and light spread where shadows had ruled.

Jesus calls His followers the light of the world, not because the glow originates in us, but because His life burns within us. Lamps are not lit to be hidden. They are placed where their light can be of use. Patrick's story shows what happens when grace refuses to stay private. Captives become carriers. Wounds become windows. Former enemies become neighbors welcomed into the mercy of Christ. The green that fills our streets each March hints at resurrection life. As winter loosens its grip, creation preaches renewal. What was buried begins to rise. In Lent, we remember that God is growing newness beneath the soil of obedience, even before the first shoot breaks the surface.

Most of us will not cross seas, but all of us are sent. The kingdom advances in ordinary rooms through steady, visible faith. Choose truth when compromise would be easier. Bless those who have not blessed you. Pray when panic wants the last word. Speak the name of Jesus with gentleness and courage. Light does not argue with darkness. It shines, and darkness loses ground. When you place your lamp on its stand, using whatever influence you have for love, your deeds become signposts that point beyond you so that others glorify your Father in heaven. The aim of shining is not applause for the lamp. It is attention for the Light.

Wear the green if you like, but walk in the grace it suggests. Let Christ's love be visible in your choices, your words, your generosity, and your forgiveness. Someone nearby is watching for a small light to help them find the way home.

Encouragement:

Your light, kindled by Christ, carries farther than you think. Even small faithfulness can warm a cold room.

Reflection:

Where is God calling you to shine more intentionally for Him this week, and what visible action of love will you take there: at home, at work, or among friends?

Notes:

_____

_____

_____

_____

Shine simply. Christ in you is enough to light the way.

Prayer:

Lord, thank You for the witness of St. Patrick and for the gospel that turns captives into carriers of Your light. Place my life on the stand You choose. Fill me with courage to love, humility to serve, and boldness to name Your goodness. May those who see my life be drawn to glorify You. Amen.

Week 17:

Welcoming the True King

Introduction:

Palm Sunday begins Holy Week with a shout of Hosanna. The crowds cheered a King, but many hoped for the wrong kind of kingdom. They wanted fast change. Jesus came to bring lasting peace. Today, we welcome Him not only with words but with surrender.

Scripture:

Matthew 21:9— "The crowds that went ahead of him and those that followed shouted, 'Hosanna to the Son of David.' 'Blessed is he who comes in the name of the Lord.' 'Hosanna in the highest heaven.'"

Message:

Palms waved and cloaks covered the road as Jesus entered Jerusalem. The hope in the air was real. So were the mixed motives. The King did not ride a warhorse. He chose a donkey and fulfilled the promise of a gentle ruler who brings peace. He would conquer, not by force, but by a cross that silences condemnation and a tomb that cannot hold Him. The sign was clear. His kingdom moves by humility, truth, and servant love.

Hosanna is both praise and prayer. Save now, and we praise the One who saves. Many wanted freedom from Rome. Jesus came to free hearts from sin and fear. This day exposes my expectations. I want a Messiah who fixes what I feel the most right now. He offers Himself and invites trust in His way and in His time. Welcoming the

King means opening every gate of life to His authority. That includes schedule, speech, conflict, money, and hidden motives.

He enters the city and then the temple. He brings worship back to the Father's heart. He will soon wash feet, share the cup, and walk a path that looks like loss and ends in victory. When I lay my cloak at His feet, I release the old coverings I use for control. Pride, the need to be right, and the habit of grasping begin to loosen. Daily procession replaces a one-day parade. I learn to say, your kingdom come, not mine, and I learn to trust that His reign brings rest to people who are tired of carrying their own crowns.

Encouragement

Jesus is the King who brings peace, not pressure. His reign frees you to lay down what you were never meant to carry.

Reflection:

What concrete act of surrender will you offer Jesus the King today, and where will you invite His peace to rule first?

Notes:

_____

_____

_____

_____

Open the gates, when Jesus reigns, peace follows.

Prayer:

Lord Jesus, I welcome You as my true King. Forgive the ways I have tried to make You fit my plans. Enter the gates of my heart, reorder my loves, and teach me Your way of peace. I lay down pride and control and receive Your gentle rule. Amen.

Week 18:

He Is Risen, Hope Lives

Introduction:

Easter is the heartbeat of our faith. The empty tomb tells the world that hope is alive because Jesus is alive. The resurrection is not only a moment in history. It is the ground under every promise God has made.

Scripture:

Matthew 28:6— "He is not here; he has risen, just as he said. Come and see the place where he lay."

Message:

At first light, the women carried spices to a sealed tomb. They had love, grief, and a practical worry about the stone. God had already moved what they could not move. The announcement was simple and world-changing. He is not here. He has risen. The cross showed love poured out. The empty tomb showed love stronger than death. The resurrection is not a private feeling. It is the Father's Yes to the finished work of the Son.

Because Jesus lives, His words can be trusted, and His forgiveness is effective. The earliest disciples did not rally around an idea. They met the risen Lord. Fearful hearts became witnesses. Locked doors opened to courage. Ordinary people began to carry news that still changes lives. Easter turns endings into beginnings and graves into gateways.

For us, resurrection is an anchor and engine. Anchor, because our hope does not rest on changing outcomes. It rests on a living Christ. Engine, because the same power that raised Jesus is at work in us. Shame points to past failure. We point to an empty tomb. Sorrow hangs like a heavy fog. The Gardener calls us by name, and we rise to follow. Death stands like a final wall. In Christ, it is a broken gate that will not hold forever.

Easter also sends us. Come and see becomes go and tell. We step into places that look sealed and speak life. We forgive as people who have been forgiven. We serve as people who have been raised. Sunday has come, and the risen Jesus still stands in the midst and says, Peace be with you.

Encouragement

Take heart. Your hope is alive because Jesus is alive. No stone is too heavy for the hands that left the grave.

Reflection:

Where does the truth of the resurrection need to speak courage into your life today, and what step of trust will follow?

Notes:

_____

_____

_____

_____

Lift your eyes, dawn has broken, the stone is moved, and hope lives in Him.

Prayer:

Risen Lord, thank You for rolling away despair and filling my life with living hope. When fear is loud, remind me that You reign. Teach me to walk in resurrection life with joy, courage, and love, and to bear faithful witness to the empty tomb. Amen.

Week 19:

The Road to Emmaus

Introduction:

The resurrection was not only witnessed. It was encountered. Two disciples walked with heavy hearts and did not recognize the risen Jesus beside them. As He opened the Scriptures and broke bread, their sorrow turned to burning joy. He still walks with us and opens our eyes to His living Presence.

Scripture:

Luke 24:32— "They asked each other, 'Were not our hearts burning within us while he talked with us on the road and opened the Scriptures to us?'"

Message:

Emmaus begins with disappointment. Two followers left Jerusalem with facts in their minds and grief in their steps. Jesus came alongside as a companion before He was known as the Lord. He asked what troubled them, listened to their story, and then opened the Scriptures from Moses through the Prophets to show how it all pointed to Him. Notice the order. He draws near. He opens the Word. Their hearts begin to burn even before their eyes can see.

This is still His way. He joins our ordinary roads and teaches us to read the Bible as one story that resolves in Christ. When we open Scripture, we are not hunting phrases. We are meeting a Person. Promises that felt distant become steady when we see them fulfilled in Jesus' life, death, and resurrection. Doubt loses ground not only by argument but by encounter. The living Word unveils the written word, and faith wakes up.

At a simple table, bread is taken, blessed, and broken. In that grace, their eyes open. Presence is recognized in the ordinary. We often look for God in dramatic signs. He delights to reveal Himself in a shared meal, a quiet prayer, or a timely line from Scripture. Hospitality becomes a holy place. When we invite Jesus to stay, He makes Himself known and changes our direction.

Emmaus ends with movement. Though night has fallen, they rise and return to Jerusalem. Encounter becomes witness. Burning hearts become willing feet. The same Lord walks with us today. He warms our hearts by His Word, makes Himself known in simple grace, and sends us back to our people with good news.

Encouragement:

You may not see Him at first, but He is walking with you. His voice can turn weary miles into holy ground.

Reflection:

How will you linger with Jesus this week so that your heart burns again in His Word and your steps carry good news back to others?

Notes:

Keep walking, He is nearer than you think, and His Presence turns the road into joy.

Prayer:

Lord Jesus, thank You for drawing near on my ordinary roads. Open the Scriptures to me and open my eyes to You. Let my heart burn with living hope and let my table be a place of Your Presence. Send me to share what you have shown. Amen.

Week 20:

Breakfast with Jesus

Introduction:

Failure can make us feel unfit to follow Christ. Peter knew that pain. After bold promises, he denied Jesus three times. The risen Lord did not discard him. He met him by the water, not with condemnation but with restoration. Grace is greater than failure, and the call still stands.

Scripture:

John 21:12, 15— "Jesus said to them, 'Come and have breakfast.' … When they had finished eating, Jesus said to Simon Peter, 'Simon son of John, do you love me more than these?'"

Message:

Dawn settled over the lake as a voice called from the shore. The disciples had fished all night and caught nothing. At the stranger's word, they cast the net again, and it filled to the edge of breaking. John knew it was the Lord. Peter dove into the water. On the beach, a charcoal fire glowed, bread and fish were ready, and the invitation all of us needed was spoken. Come and have breakfast.

The scene is filled with mercy. Peter's denial had happened near another charcoal fire. Now, beside a new one, Jesus rewrites the memory. He begins with hospitality rather than accusation. He serves a meal before He asks a question. After they eat, Jesus turns to Peter. Three times He asks, Do you love Me. Three answers draw Peter out of regret and back into calling. Feed My lambs. Tend My sheep. Feed

My sheep. Love becomes the qualification, not flawless performance.

This is the shape of restoration. Jesus does not pretend the failure never happened. He redeems it. He folds the place of collapse into the work ahead. The full net hints at the future. Their strength will not carry their mission. It will overflow with His. By the end, the first command that ever called Peter sounds again. Follow Me. It is as if Jesus says that His plan for Peter was never in danger.

When we fail, Jesus meets us at the shoreline, not the courthouse. He invites us to sit, to be fed, to answer truthfully, and to hear purpose spoken again. Restoration grows through simple steps. Confess what you hid. Receive the forgiveness you cannot earn. Make amends where you can. Care for the people in front of you. The fire is warm. The invitation stands. His call still finds you.

Encouragement:

Your failure is not the headline of your story. Jesus' forgiveness is. The same Lord who called you at first calls you again today.

Reflection:

Where do you need to sit by His fire, receive His mercy, and take one step back into the work He has entrusted to you?

Notes

_____

_____

_____

_____

Take heart—the fire is warm, the invitation stands, and His call still finds you on the shore.

Prayer:

Lord Jesus, thank You for meeting me where I fell and feeding me with grace. Rewrite my memories with Your mercy. I say yes to Your love and Your call. Lead me from regret into restoration and from shame into faithful service. Amen.

Week 21:

He Believes in You

Introduction:

It is my sincere hope, and even more, it is God's heart, that every person would come to know Jesus Christ as Lord and Savior. There is nothing more important or more lasting than where we will spend eternity. Your eternal address matters, and God has prepared a place for you in His kingdom. The invitation is open. The door is Christ. He stands ready to receive you. If you feel far or uncertain, hear this: even if you struggle to believe in God, He remains faithful to you. His love does not waver. His mercy does not fail. The time to turn toward Him is now.

Scripture:

2 Timothy 2:13— "If we are faithless, he remains faithful, for he cannot disown himself."

Message:

There is a comforting truth folded into grace. God's faithfulness is not a mirror that reflects our performance. It is a fountain that flows from His unchanging character. When Paul writes, "If we are faithless, He remains faithful," he anchors hope not in our grip on God but in God's grip on us. The Lord does not redefine Himself by our doubts. He does not cancel compassion when our courage runs thin. He remains faithful because faithfulness is who He is.

Scripture is full of people who hesitated or resisted and were met by persistent mercy. Moses questioned his calling, and God met him with Presence. Peter denied Jesus, and the risen Lord restored him by a charcoal fire and recommissioned him. Saul hunted the church, and Christ confronted him on the road and turned a persecutor into a preacher. In every story, God's steadfast love moved first. He saw what they could become in His hands and called them into it.

When we say God believes in you, we do not mean He overlooks sin. We mean He is committed to His purpose for you. He sees you as His image bearer, calls you by name, and invites you into new life in Christ. His covenant faithfulness is His promise to complete what He begins. He knows the gap between who you are and who you were made to be, and He bridges it through the cross and the empty tomb.

If faith feels out of reach, start where the gospel starts, with God's faithful love. You can bring Him your unbelief without disguise. You can whisper, "Lord, I believe. Help my unbelief," and find that His patience is longer than your questions. Turn to Jesus as you are. Confess sin. Receive forgiveness. Ask the Spirit to awaken trust. Faith often grows by a step. Open the Scriptures. Pray a simple prayer. Reach out to a believer who will walk with you. As you respond, you will find the One drawing you has been near all along.

Encouragement:

Even in your unbelief, God's faithfulness holds steady. He is not done writing your story.

Reflection:

Have you considered that God's faithful love reaches for you before you reach for Him? What response will you make to that love today?

Notes:

_____

_____

_____

_____

Take courage—His faithfulness is already reaching for you, and His arms are open wide.

Prayer:

Father, thank You for loving me when my faith is small and my doubts feel large. Thank You that Your character does not change with my feelings. Today I turn toward You. Forgive my sin, heal my heart, and make me new in Christ. Teach me to trust Your promises and to walk in the purpose You have for me. My life is Yours. In Jesus' name, amen.

Week 22:

Living in Resurrection Hope

Introduction:

There are seasons when hope feels fragile, as if we are trying to hold it rather than it holding us. But the hope we have in Christ is not flimsy or distant. It is alive. It anchors us. It was born the moment Jesus walked out of the tomb.

Scripture:

1 Peter 1:3— "Praise be to the God and Father of our Lord Jesus Christ. In his great mercy, he has given us new birth into a living hope through the resurrection of Jesus Christ from the dead."

Message:

Peter calls it living hope because it shares its life with a living Lord. This hope is not wishful thinking that rises and falls with circumstances. It is a new life born in us by God's mercy and tied to a historical resurrection that cannot be undone. Scattered believers faced trial and misunderstanding, yet Peter begins with praise. Hope starts not with our grip on God but with God's grace toward us. He has given us new birth.

Living hope has a source, a scope, and a staying power. Its source is the resurrection. Jesus truly died, truly rose, and now reigns. Because He lives, our worst verdicts are not our final chapters. Shame yields to forgiveness. Futility yields to purpose. Death yields to life. Its scope reaches into our present and our future. Our inheritance is kept in heaven, and God's power keeps us through faith. Hope is not a fragile capital we must guard. It is safeguarded by the God who raised Jesus.

Its staying power appears in the furnace. Trials refine faith like fire purifies gold, so that praise and honor will be given to Christ. Living hope does not require us to pretend the fire is cool. It promises the flame will not have the last word. Even when we do not see Him, we love Him. Even now, we believe and are filled with a joy beyond words, receiving the salvation of our souls.

This hope is not self-generated zeal. It is an inherited life. The same power that raised Christ now works toward us who believe. When grief lingers or answers delay, we do not force optimism. We lean into the risen Christ. We pray honestly, obey steadily, and wait expectantly. Resurrection is not only behind us as an event. It is within us by His Spirit and before us as a promise.

Encouragement:

Resurrection did not just happen. By His Spirit, it is happening. The Jesus who rose still raises.

Reflection:

Where do you need to remember that hope is alive because Christ is alive, and how will trusting His resurrection power steady you there today?

Notes:

Take heart—because Jesus lives, hope holds.

Prayer:

Lord, thank You for the living hope I have through the resurrection of Jesus. When I grow weary, remind me that my hope is anchored in Your victory. Steady my heart in trial, renew my courage to obey, and breathe Your life into what feels buried. Let my days bear witness to the power of the risen Christ. Amen.

Week 23:

The Lord Is My Shepherd

Introduction:

Every one of us follows a shepherd. For some, it is money, success, relationships, or our own desires. A shepherd is what leads us, guides decisions, and shapes direction. The question is not whether we have a shepherd. The question is, who is your shepherd?

Scripture:

Psalm 23:1— "The Lord is my shepherd; I shall not want."

Message:

David opens with a confession that is both intimate and bold. The Lord is my shepherd. Not a shepherd in theory, but mine in covenant care. In one sentence, our lives move from self-reliance to divine provision. Sheep without a shepherd wander and exhaust themselves. Under a true shepherd they are led, guarded, and named. I shall not want does not deny real need. It declares that lack will not be the master of a life held by God.

Watch how the psalm moves. He makes me lie down in green pastures. He leads me beside still waters. He restores my soul. Grace sets the pace. The Shepherd initiates, and the sheep receive. Rest is not a reward for performance but a gift from

Presence. He guides in paths of righteousness for His name's sake. His own character binds Him to faithful leadership. He stakes His reputation on our care.

The scene darkens. Though I walk through the valley of the shadow of death, I will fear no evil, for You are with me. Shadows loom, but they have no substance where the Light is near. The rod defends and the staff directs, and together they comfort. We do not sprint through the valley. We are escorted.

Then comes a surprise. You prepare a table before me in the Presence of my enemies. God's answer to hostility is hospitality. He not only removes threats, He nourishes us while they watch. Anointing our heads with oil until the cup overflows. In Christ the Good Shepherd, this song finds its fullest voice. He sought us when we strayed, laid down His life, and rose to keep us forever. Goodness and mercy will pursue us all our days, and the journey ends at home in the house of the Lord.

Encouragement:

You do not wander alone. Your Shepherd is near, His rod defends, His staff directs, and His table never runs dry.

Reflection:

Who or what most tries to shepherd your steps, and what choice this week will place your pace and plans under the Shepherd's voice?

Notes:

Lift your eyes—where He leads, provision and peace await.

Prayer

Lord, thank You for being my Shepherd. Forgive me when I chase lesser guides. Lead me to green pastures and still waters, restore my soul, and guide me for Your name's sake. When valleys darken, steady me with Your Presence. Let goodness and mercy pursue me, and keep me near Your house forever. Amen.

Week 24:

God's Healing Touch

Introduction:

The Gospels are filled with Jesus healing the sick, restoring sight, and making the lame walk. These were not side notes. They revealed the heart of God. Jesus welcomed the hurting and did not turn them away.

Scripture:

Matthew 15:30— "Great crowds came to him, bringing the lame, the blind, the crippled, the mute, and many others, and laid them at his feet; and he healed them."

Message:

Crowds carried their pain to Jesus and laid it at His feet. The scene is tender and powerful. Need moves toward mercy, and mercy moves toward need. Matthew writes without qualifiers, and He healed them. There is no triage at the door, no screening for worthiness. The compassion of Christ does not flinch at broken bodies or burdened hearts. He receives, He touches, and He makes whole.

Scripture often joins forgiveness and healing in one breath. He forgives all your sins and heals all your diseases. In Jesus, the kingdom has drawn near. Sin is pardoned, shame is lifted, and the works of the evil one are undone. The cross shows love that bears our deepest sickness. The empty tomb declares life that is stronger than death. Our hope for healing rests not in our power to believe but in

His faithful character. Jesus Christ is the same yesterday, today, and forever.

How do we come to Him? We come honestly, naming our wounds and refusing to carry them alone. We come expectantly, because nothing is impossible with God. We also come surrendered, trusting His wisdom in the way He heals. Sometimes He acts suddenly. Sometimes slowly. Sometimes, He gives sustaining grace in the trial. Often, He works through the good gifts of medicine, counselors, and community. Healing is both a sign and a promise. It points to the kingdom that is already here, and to the day when every tear will be wiped away and every body raised imperishable.

So bring what hurts. Bring the diagnosis and the disappointment, the grief you cannot voice, and the ache you barely admit. Lay them at His feet in prayer, and invite others to carry you with their prayers too. The first movement is always His. Christ is moving toward you with compassion that does not grow tired.

Encouragement:

Jesus welcomes the wounded and meets them with mercy. His Presence is near, and His power has not diminished.

Reflection:

Where do you need the touch of Jesus today in body, mind, or soul, and what will it look like to place that need at His feet with trust?

Notes:

Take heart—your need is not ignored; His hands are open, and His heart is kind.

Prayer:

Lord Jesus, thank You for Your compassion and Your power to heal. I bring You what is broken in me and around me. Touch what I cannot fix, strengthen me where I am weak, and guide me in every step of care and obedience. Let Your peace guard my heart as I trust Your faithful love. Amen.

Week 25:
Abiding in the True Vine

Introduction:

Life pulls us in many directions. Work, family, responsibility, and even ministry tug on our attention. In the rush, it is easy to start operating on our own strength. Jesus gives us a clear picture of how we are meant to live: connected, dependent, and rooted in Him. Just as a branch cannot survive apart from the vine, our lives cannot flourish apart from His Presence.

Scripture:

John 15:5— "I am the vine; you are the branches. If you remain in me and I in you, you will bear much fruit; apart from me you can do nothing."

Message:

On the night before the cross, Jesus did not hand His friends a strategy. He offered a relationship. "I am the vine; you are the branches." The image is tender and uncompromising. Branches do not siphon life from themselves; they receive it. Their fruit is not the outcome of anxiety but of attachment. Abiding is Jesus' way of saying that closeness is not optional for discipleship. It is the very atmosphere of it.

Abiding is not passivity. It is a lived reliance that shows up in ordinary rhythms. His words settle into our minds and reorder our inner conversations. Our prayers rise from dependence rather than panic. Our obedience flows from love rather than fear. As His life circulates through ours, the symptoms of self-reliance begin to fade. Exhaustion gives way to renewal because strength is drawn, not manufactured. Identity steadies because worth is received, not negotiated with circumstances or opinions. Desire is purified because the sap of the vine carries new appetites into old branches. Over time, we notice that the fruit others taste from our lives is joy, peace, patience, kindness, goodness, faithfulness, gentleness, and self-control. These are not decorations we tape to the branch. They are the natural produce of remaining in Jesus.

Jesus' blunt phrase, "apart from me you can do nothing," is not a threat. It is liberation. It releases us from the exhausting fiction that results depend on our hustle. We are not the vine, and the world is not waiting for our brilliance to bloom. Fruitfulness is the Spirit's quiet miracle in a heart that remains. As we stay, even our prayers begin to change. Requests align with His heart. His promises shape petitions. Intercession grows patient because love abides. Where striving once squeezed fruit from duty, abiding grows it from delight.

Pruning is part of this love. The Vinedresser removes what siphons life so that more life can flow. Pruning can feel like subtraction, but it is actually preparation for abundance. Seasons of less noise or fewer distractions often become seasons of more holiness, more clarity, and deeper joy. The knife is in a Father's hand. No cut is careless. Nothing truly fruitful is lost, and nothing truly harmful is kept.

So we practice staying near. We linger in Scripture long enough for it to linger in us. We tell Jesus the truth instead of performing a prayer. We choose obedience in small, hidden places and trust that roots deepen before branches heavy with fruit appear. Abiding is not glamorous. It is steady. Yet in this steadiness, the life of the True Vine flows, and fruit follows in its time.

Encouragement:

You were never meant to do life alone. Stay with the Vine. He will supply what you cannot.

Reflection:

Where have you been trying to produce visible results without drawing invisible life from Jesus, and how will you turn toward Him to receive rather than strive today?

Notes:

_____

_____

_____

_____

Hold fast—His life in you will bear what your effort never could.

Prayer:

Lord, teach me to abide in You. Settle Your word in my heart, quiet my striving, and let Your life flow through every part of me. Prune what hinders love. Strengthen what bears Your likeness. Make my days fruitful for Your glory and full of Your joy. Amen.

Week 26:

Spirit's Call to Witness

Introduction:

Every gift God gives comes with purpose. The Holy Spirit does not rest on us only for personal comfort or private devotion. He empowers us to step into a calling bigger than ourselves.

Scripture:

Isaiah 61:1–2— "The Spirit of the Sovereign Lord is on me, because the Lord has anointed me to proclaim good news to the poor. He has sent me to bind up the broken-hearted, to proclaim freedom for the captives and release from darkness for the prisoners, to proclaim the year of the Lord's favor…"

Message:

Isaiah's prophecy is not abstract poetry. It is a mission statement. When Jesus unrolled the scroll in Nazareth and read these very words, He finished with a startling claim. "Today this Scripture is fulfilled in your hearing." In Christ, the promised announcement arrived. The poor heard good news. The broken-hearted felt the binding of mercy. Captives tasted freedom, and those sitting in darkness saw great light. The same Jesus who fulfilled Isaiah 61 now pours out His Spirit on His people, not to make us spectators but participants. The Spirit that rested on Him rests on us, so that His ministry continues through ordinary lives yielded to extraordinary grace.

To be anointed is to be appointed. The Spirit's Presence is not spiritual decor. It is divine enablement. He consoles us in our sorrows, and He also commissions us out of them. We are comforted in order to become comforters. We are forgiven in order to extend forgiveness. We are set free in order to speak freedom. The assignment is not reserved for the eloquent or the prominent. It flows from belonging to Jesus. Oil once marked kings and priests. The Spirit now marks sons and daughters. Wherever you find poverty of Spirit, heaviness of heart, chains of shame, or rooms dimmed by despair, you have stepped onto the ground Isaiah described, and the Spirit in you is adequate for it.

What does this look like in the fabric of a week? A conversation shifts when you name the hope of Christ with gentleness and clarity. A wound begins to mend when you sit with a grieving friend and ask the Healer to draw near. A burden lifts when you intercede for someone who cannot find words, trusting the Spirit to help in weakness. A quiet act of justice, a faithful word of truth, and a patient choice to forgive become living proclamations of the Lord's favor. In those moments, you are not trying to be impressive. You are simply carrying what you have received.

You are not sent alone. The Spirit who sends also sustains. The weight of changed hearts never sits on your shoulders. Your role is witness, not savior. Your task is lamp, not sun. The anointing does not inflate the ego. It enlarges love. It teaches us to move at Jesus' pace and in Jesus' manner, humble, gentle, courageous, and kind. If you feel inadequate, remember that "the Spirit of the Sovereign Lord is on me" is not a boast but a confession of dependence. Lean there, then take the next obedient step and trust the Lord with the outcome.

Encouragement:

You are anointed for this. The Spirit who fills you is the One who sends you and stays with you.

Reflection:

Where might the Holy Spirit be inviting you to carry hope, healing, or freedom to someone this week, and what simple act of obedient love will you take?

Notes:

_____

_____

_____

_____

Go in confidence—the One who sends you walks beside you and works through you.

Prayer:

Holy Spirit, thank You for anointing me with purpose. Open my eyes to the poor in Spirit and the broken-hearted around me. Put Your word on my tongue, Your compassion in my hands, and Your courage in my steps. Let my life proclaim Your favor, and use me to bring freedom and light in Jesus' name. Amen.

Week 27:

Living Water and Thirsting for God

Introduction:

Every heart carries a thirst, an ache for meaning, fulfillment, relief, or connection. We chase satisfaction in accomplishments, relationships, routines, or escape, but the longing always returns. Jesus does not condemn that hunger; He redirects it. He reminds us that thirst is not a flaw to hide but an invitation to come.

Scripture:

John 4:13–14— "Jesus answered, 'Everyone who drinks this water will be thirsty again, but whoever drinks the water I give them will never thirst. Indeed, the water I give them will become in them a spring of water welling up to eternal life.'"

Message:

She came at noon when the heat keeps others away. Shame prefers empty paths and silent wells. Yet Jesus chose that hour and that road, waiting where her avoidance had led her. He began, not with accusation, but with a request: "Will you give me a drink?" He was not thirsty for water so much as ready to draw her heart to grace. Beneath the routine of filling a jar, He named a deeper lack that no earthen vessel could hold.

The woman had learned to live from temporary sources. Relationships promised belonging but kept breaking. The jar went down and came up, again and again, and still she was parched. Jesus redirected her gaze from the depth of Jacob's well to the Gift standing before her. "If you knew the gift of God…" He offered not a technique but Himself, living water that does more than satisfy for a moment. It becomes a spring within, rising with a life no drought can drain.

This is the difference between wells and springs. A well depends on where you dig and how strong you feel today. A spring depends on the source beneath the surface. We often try to manage thirst with achievement, distraction, or approval, but these are seasonal cisterns that crack under pressure. Christ does not shame our longing. He sanctifies it, turning thirst into a homing signal that leads us back to Him. To drink the water, He gives is not a single sip of inspiration but a new birth into a life where His Spirit makes the heart a fountain. Prayer begins to flow where anxiety once pooled. Forgiveness wells up where resentment had settled. Praise rises where despair had grown quiet roots.

Jesus spoke plainly: "Apart from me you can do nothing." That is not a scold. It is liberation for the weary. We do not have to manufacture meaning or wring refreshment from dry ground. We come, we ask, we receive. As we keep company with Christ, letting His word dwell in us, bringing our honest thirst to Him,

opening our hands where we once clenched them, the stream strengthens. She left her jar and ran to tell others. When living water takes residence, it does not stagnate; it overflows.

If your soul feels sun-beaten and your steps avoid the crowds, hear Jesus' kindness at the well. Come to Him and drink. With that invitation fresh in our ears, let us turn to reflection and name the lesser wells we are ready to leave behind.

Encouragement:

Jesus does not only quench thirst, but by His Spirit, He becomes a spring within you.

Reflection:

Where have you been drawing from wells that never satisfy, and how will you turn toward Jesus to drink deeply of His living water today?

Notes:

_____

_____

_____

_____

Come and drink—His living water is enough for today and more than enough for tomorrow.

Prayer:

Lord, I bring You the dry ground of my heart. I confess to the lesser wells I keep returning to. Teach me to come to You, to receive the gift of Your Presence, and to live from the spring You place within me. Refresh my soul, renew my desires, and let Your life overflow to others. Amen.

Week 28: Strength in Stillness

Introduction:

There are moments in life when movement feels like the only answer. Problems loom, emotions rise, and silence feels unproductive. Yet some of God's greatest works are not found in our striving but in our stillness. Stillness is not inactivity. It is intentional trust. It is choosing to pause long enough to recognize that God is present, powerful, and in control.

Scripture:

Psalm 46:10— "Be still, and know that I am God…"

Message:

Psalm 46 is written for shaking days. Nations rage, mountains crumble, waters roar. Everything that felt permanent trembles. Yet the psalm begins with a declaration, not a description: "God is our refuge and strength, an ever-present help in trouble." In that context, the command arrives: "Be still, and know that I am God." The Hebrew behind "be still" carries the sense of relax, let go, release your grip. "Know" is more than information; it is recognition born of relationship. Together they form a holy posture: loosen what you cannot hold and lean into the One who holds you.

Stillness is not passivity; it is reorientation. When I stop rehearsing every worst-case scenario and set my mind on who God is, peace finds a foothold. He is the Lord of hosts who makes wars cease. He is the God in our midst who will not let us fall. Isaiah echoes, "In quietness and trust is your strength," not because quiet solves problems but because trust roots us in the God who does. The story of Israel at the Red Sea gives this stillness a scene. The sea was ahead, an army behind, terror rising in the throat, and then the word, "The Lord will fight for you; you need only to be still." Stillness there was not quitting. It was refusing to let panic captain the moment while God opened a path no eye could see.

Elijah learned the same lesson on the mountain. Wind shattered rocks, an earthquake shook the ground, fire blazed, and God came in none of them. Then a gentle whisper. The voice was always present. Hurry was too loud to hear it. Stillness creates the quiet where assurance can be received. It loosens my clenched plans and lets God's Presence become the strength beneath my feet. Some breakthroughs do not come by force but by rest. Some answers arrive not in our rush but in our pause. We work when it is time to work. We move when God says go. We begin with surrender: You are God; I am not.

"Be still" is not an escape from responsibility; it is an exit from fear. It is choosing to trust God more than my timeline, my calculation, and my need to control outcomes. In the quiet, strength rises, not because I have found more within myself, but because I have found Him. When He is known, peace becomes possible even before circumstances change. From that place, let us name where He is inviting us to lay down our striving and rest in His strength.

Encouragement:

Your stillness is not weakness. It is trust in motion, making space for God to be God.

Reflection:

Where might God be inviting you to stop striving and rest in His strength, and what would practicing stillness look like in that specific place today?

Notes:

_____

_____

_____

_____

Be still—He is here, and His Presence is stronger than the storm.

Prayer

Lord, calm my anxious heart. Teach me to release what I cannot carry and to rest in who You are. Let Your Presence quiet my fears, Your word steady my steps, and Your strength become my song. I choose to be still and know that You are God over every detail of my life. Amen.

Week 29:
Faith Over Fear

Introduction:

Fear is a quiet thief that creeps into the corners of our hearts. It whispers doubts about our worth, our future, and our ability to face the unknown. Often, it disguises itself as practicality or caution, convincing us that worry is preparation. Yet the Lord calls us to a higher path, a path where faith triumphs over fear, where trust in His character and promises eclipses the shadows of anxiety.

Scripture:

Isaiah 41:10— "So do not fear, for I am with you, do not be dismayed, for I am your God. I will strengthen you and help you, I will uphold you with my righteous right hand."

Message:

Fear is woven into the human story, but it is not the headline of God's story. Isaiah's words were first spoken to a people facing pressure from powers they could not match. Into their tremor, God did not offer technique; He offered Himself. Notice the cadence. I am with you. I am your God. I will strengthen you. I will help you. I will uphold you. The antidote to fear is not a louder inner voice; it is a nearer God. Faith grows where the Presence of God moves from concept to company.

"Do not fear" is not a scolding; it is an invitation anchored in relationship. We are told not to fear because someone stronger has taken our hand. God's love does not mock our shakiness; it meets it.

When the psalmist testifies, "I sought the Lord, and he answered me, he delivered me from all my fears" (Psalm 34:4), deliverance begins in the seeking. Fear narrows our gaze to the problem, faith lifts our eyes to the Person who holds us. The problem may remain, but it loses the power to define the moment when God's nearness defines us instead.

Faith over fear does not mean we feel nothing; it means we relocate our weight. We shift it from our outcomes to His character, from our control to His covenant. The God who says, "I am your God," binds His name to our care. He strengthens when our resolve thins, helps when our wisdom ends, and upholds when our footing fails. The righteous right hand is a picture of power used in love, steady, sufficient, and unfailing. Even the cross speaks into our fears. In Christ, the worst has already been met by the love of God and overturned by the power of resurrection. If death itself could not hold Him, then no present threat holds final authority over those in His hand.

Practically, faith takes the next faithful step. We breathe and name our fear before God instead of letting it rule in silence. We answer fear's lies with Scripture's truth. You are with me. We ask for the Spirit's courage to act in obedience while our knees still shake. And we remember that grace is not only pardon for sin, it is power for the fearful heart. God's help is not occasional charity; it is daily bread. As we keep company with Him, fear's volume lowers and trust's melody grows steady.

So listen again to the promise, I am with you. Let those words be the ground beneath your feet. With that assurance, we turn toward reflection and invite His peace to lead where fear once lingered.

Encouragement:

God's strength is greater than your fears. His hand is steady, and it is holding you now.

Reflection:

Where is fear quietly influencing your decisions or stealing your peace, and how might God's promise, I am with you, I will uphold you, reshape your next step?

Notes:

_____

_____

_____

_____

Take heart—His hand is under you, and His Presence goes before you

Prayer

Father, I choose faith over fear. Thank You that You are with me and that You are my God. Strengthen me where I am weak, help me where I am unsure, and uphold me when I feel unsteady. Let Your promises quiet my anxiety and Your Presence lead me forward in peace. In Jesus' name, amen.

Week 30:

When God's "Never" Is Always

Introduction:

Some words can drain the life from us: never good enough, never going to change, never going to make it. But there is a holy "never" that reverses every discouraging echo. God's "never" is not a ceiling; it is a covenant. In a world of shifting vows and fragile promises, His "never" is your "always."

Scripture:

Hebrews 13:5 — "Never will I leave you; never will I forsake you."

Message:

There are days when faith feels thin, when prayers seem to hover just above our heads, and the silence of God feels heavier than the words we can muster. In moments like these, our feelings try to tell the story. But God's Word does not run on emotion; it runs on promise. He does not make casual statements; He makes covenants. The Author of your life has already bound Himself to you with a vow that cannot be revoked: "Never will I leave you; never will I forsake you."

To say "never" is to settle the question before it is asked. The Lord is not gauging your worthiness to decide whether He will stay close. He is not partly in and partly out, waiting for a reason to withdraw. In Christ, He has tied His Presence to you with an unbreakable bond, sealed by His blood, affirmed by His Spirit, and anchored in His character. When you stumble, He does not step back. When you doubt, He does not distance Himself. When you feel alone, He is nearer than breath, faithful to His own name.

Scripture keeps circling this truth so we will not forget it. God promises never to break His covenant (Judges 2:1). Jesus assures that whoever comes to Him will never be cast out (John 6:37). The righteous are described as never shaken because their footing is in God, not in circumstance (Psalm 112:6). And love, God's love, never fails (1 Corinthians 13:8). These are not soft hopes or wishful intentions; they are guaranteed realities that rest on who He is.

Let His "never" speak louder than the fog of feeling. Feelings can be real and still be unreliable. God's Word is both real and unchanging. Let it steady your steps when the road feels uncertain. Whisper truth over your heart: I am never abandoned. Christ is with me in this room, in this decision, in this ache, in this joy. The promise still stands, and the Promise-Keeper still reigns. Lean into that certainty, and let it carry you from fear to trust, from striving to rest, because His "never" is your "always."

Encouragement:

You are not walking toward God's Presence; you are walking with it. When feelings get loud, remember that His "never" is louder. He has not moved, and His promise still holds.

Reflection:

Where have your feelings grown louder than God's promise never to leave you, and what will you do differently this week because He is truly with you?

Notes:

_____

_____

_____

_____

Take a breath and listen. His faithful "never" is speaking over you even now.

Prayer:

Father, thank You for a promise that does not bend with my emotions. When doubt whispers, remind me that I am never alone. When fear tightens its grip, let Your Word loosen it with truth. Teach me to live today with calm confidence in Your nearness. In Jesus' name, amen.

Week 31:

The Power of Gentle Words

Introduction:

Words have power; they can build up or tear down, encourage or discourage, heal or hurt. In a world where harsh speech is often normalized and immediate reactions are expected, gentleness in our words can feel countercultural. Yet Scripture reminds us that the way we speak can reflect God's heart, influence our relationships, and even shape our own inner peace.

Scripture:

Proverbs 15:1— "A gentle answer turns away wrath, but a harsh word stirs up anger."

Message

Proverbs 15:1 gives us more than communication advice; it offers a spiritual principle. Gentle words do not ignore truth; they deliver it in a way the heart can receive. A gentle answer is not timidity or evasion; it is strength under control and wisdom harnessed by love. Harshness may win quick compliance, but it rarely forms lasting change. Gentleness lowers defenses, invites reflection, and clears space for God to work.

Jesus models this perfectly. He could be unflinchingly firm and yet profoundly tender. To Mary in the garden, a single word, her name, opened her eyes to resurrection hope. To the woman caught in adultery, He spoke truth without humiliation, "Neither do I condemn you, go now and leave your life of sin." His words never traded integrity for niceness, nor compassion for bluntness; they braided both. Even His rebukes carried redemptive intent, guiding people toward freedom rather than shaming them into silence.

Gentle speech reshapes our inner world as well. James warns that the tongue is small but powerful, capable of setting the course of a life on fire. When we choose gentleness, we not only de-escalate the room, but we also de-escalate our own soul. The Spirit cultivates patience in us as we slow down, listen, and answer from peace rather than from wounded pride. Over time, gentleness becomes a reflex that grows from a heart at rest in God's love.

Practically, gentleness begins before we speak. It looks like pausing long enough to pray, "Lord, lead my words," then listening to understand rather than to win. It sounds like truth wrapped in empathy, "I care about you and what you are feeling; here is what I am seeing." It asks questions that invite rather than accusations that corner. It resists exaggerations and labels that inflame, and it remembers that every person bears the image of God, even when we disagree.

Encouragement:

A gentle word can carry the weight of heaven. It calms storms, opens hearts, and reflects God's love where it is most needed.
Reflection:

Where could gentleness in your speech transform a relationship or bring peace, and what would a gentle answer sound like in that setting this week?

Notes:

_____

_____

_____

_____

Speak softly with Spirit-given strength—your words can become a doorway for God's peace.

Prayer:

Lord, teach me to speak with gentleness and grace. Place a guard over my lips and a calm within my heart. Let my words carry truth without harm, courage without contempt, and love without compromise. Use my speech to heal, to build, and to bless. Amen.

Week 32:

Doing the Right Thing, Even When Others Are Not

Introduction:

It is easy to be kind to kind people and patient with those who are patient with us. When we meet harshness, dismissal, or disrespect, something in us wants to mirror it back. That is when faith is tested. Jesus did not tell us to treat others the way they treat us. He told us to treat others the way we long to be treated. One is reaction; the other is righteousness.

Scripture:

Matthew 7:12—"So in everything, do to others what you would have them do to you, for this sums up the Law and the Prophets."

Message:

Following Christ means we act from principle rather than from the heat of our emotions. When we are wronged, our instincts shout, defend yourself, fire back, pull away. Scripture reorders our reflexes. Do not repay anyone evil for evil. Do not be overcome by evil, but overcome evil with good. This does not minimize injustice or call us to silence in the face of harm. It calls us to respond in a way that honors God and refuses to fuel the cycle of hurt. We can stand firm without becoming bitter. We can walk in truth without abandoning grace.

Because this is not easy, we start with prayer. Before we answer a text, write an email, or rehearse our defense, we bring our frustration to the Lord. Prayer does not only calm us; it realigns us. It shifts the question from, how do I feel, to, how does Jesus want me to respond. In that turning, God changes our vision. We begin to see people not as enemies to defeat but as image bearers who may be wounded, deceived, or afraid. Hurt people often hurt people. Healed people extend healing. From the cross Jesus prayed, "Father, forgive them, for they do not know what they are doing." He saw beyond behavior to blindness and He invites us to see in the same way.

The Golden Rule is more than a polite maxim; it is a kingdom weapon. When we treat others as we wish to be treated, we are not mirroring their mood; we are reflecting Christ's heart. Grace was poured over our lives when we least deserved it. Now He asks us to pour from that same fountain. This is not weakness. It is Spirit governed strength that answers insult with blessing, sets wise boundaries without malice, and chooses integrity when compromise would be easier. Proverbs says, "The righteous lead blameless lives; blessed are their children after them." Quiet faithfulness preaches louder than our sharpest retort. Our refusal to retaliate may be the seed that softens a hard heart.

So today we choose righteousness over reaction. We let Jesus set the tone, not offense. As we do, we trust that the One who sees in secret will sustain us in public and that overcoming evil with good is never wasted.

Encouragement:

You do not need permission from others to do what is right. Honor God, rise above offense, and trust that He sees and rewards every act of integrity.

Reflection:

Are you reacting to people based on how they treat you, or responding based on how Christ has treated you, and what will a Christ like response look like in one specific situation this week?

Notes:

_____

_____

_____

_____

Take heart—choosing righteousness over reaction invites God's peace into the moment.

Prayer:

Lord Jesus, when I am provoked, slow my tongue and steady my heart. Teach me to answer from Your grace rather than my grievance, to set wise and loving boundaries without malice, and to overcome evil with good. Let my responses reflect Your kindness and truth, and use my obedience to plant peace where strife once ruled. Amen.

Week 33:
Seeds of Kindness

Introduction:

In a world often focused on what we can gain, the power of small acts of love can easily be overlooked. Yet Scripture reminds us that even the tiniest seeds, when sown faithfully, can grow into a bountiful harvest. Kindness may not always bring immediate recognition, but God sees every gesture, every word, every deed done in love. It is in these seemingly small moments that His kingdom advances and hearts are transformed.

Scripture:
Galatians 6:9—"Let us not become weary in doing good, for at the proper time we will reap a harvest if we do not give up."

Message:

Paul's encouragement to the Galatians is honest about fatigue. Doing good can be tiring, especially when results seem slow and gratitude is scarce. Yet he ties perseverance to promise. There is a harvest, and it comes in God's time. Kindness is never wasted because it is never merely horizontal. It is planted in the soil of God's faithfulness. When we bless another, we lay a seed where the Lord Himself tends the ground.

Jesus loved to reveal the power of small offerings. A boy's simple lunch fed thousands because Jesus received it, blessed it, and multiplied it. A widow's two copper coins drew heaven's attention because love, not amount, measured the gift. A woman's poured out perfume seemed extravagant to some, but Jesus called it beautiful and made her quiet devotion a story told wherever the gospel goes. None of these acts would have trended in their moment. All of them became part of God's great harvest.

Kindness also works a harvest within us. As we choose mercy over indifference and encouragement over critique, our hearts become softer, our eyes quicker to notice need, and our hands readier to serve. The Father who sees what is done in secret shapes Christ like character in hidden places. Farmers do not dig up seeds to check progress. They water, wait, and trust the seasons God governs. In seasons when love is not returned or fruit is not yet visible, we remember that our kindness rests in the hands of a faithful God.

So keep sowing. Smile at the weary cashier and mean it. Write the note you have delayed. Pray a blessing over the coworker who frustrates you. Give quietly where you can. Speak courage into a child's heart. Offer a listening ear without rushing to fix. Each small seed rests in the hands of a big God, and He alone knows how far its roots will spread and how many lives its shade will one day cover.

Encouragement:

Even the tiniest seed of love can grow into a life changing harvest. Keep sowing faithfully.

Reflection:

Where will you sow a small seed of kindness this week, trusting God to water it and bring a harvest in His time?

Notes:

_____

_____

_____

_____

Keep planting, God is tending what you may not yet see.

Prayer:

Lord, make me faithful in the small things. Open my eyes to the needs around me and teach my heart to move with Your compassion. Guard me from weariness and discouragement. Receive each gesture of kindness, bless it, and bear fruit for Your kingdom in due season. In Jesus' name, amen.

Week 34:

Seeing Beyond the Giant

Introduction:

When we retell David and Goliath, we usually start with the giant's size. Israel did too, measuring height, armor, and odds. David measured something else. He named Goliath not by his stature but by his status, outside covenant with the living God. This simple shift invites us to see our own giants differently, not by how loud they loom, but by how small they stand beneath God's authority.

Scripture:

1 Samuel 17:26—"Who is this uncircumcised Philistine that he should defy the armies of the living God?"

Message:

The valley rang with taunts for forty days. Goliath's Presence was undeniable, a towering figure with bronze glinting in the sun, a spear like a weaver's beam, and a shield bearer pacing before him. Israel did the math and came up short. Fear multiplied with every shout. David took stock as well, but he did not begin with the giant, he began with God. By calling Goliath "uncircumcised," David was not slinging an insult; he was locating the contest. This opponent stood outside God's covenant, defying not merely Israel but the Lord Himself. The true imbalance was not between the warrior and the shepherd boy. It was between a creature and the Creator.

Faith does not deny facts; it defies finality. David did not pretend Goliath was small. He simply refused to let size be the story. He remembered who God is and who God's people are. Covenant means belonging, God's name upon His people, God's promises under their feet. That is why David could say, "The battle is the Lord's." When the outcome rests on God's character, intimidation loses its leverage.

Our giants have modern armor. They swagger as diagnoses, debts, addictions, rejections, headlines, and private fears in the night. They measure themselves in percentages and probabilities. Yet the question remains the same. By what authority do they defy the purposes of God in your life. If God is for us, who can be against us. This is not bravado. It is covenant logic. Giants may stand against you, but they do not stand above the Lord who is with you.

Seeing beyond the giant does not mean passivity. It means obedience. David ran to the battle line with a sling and five stones, not because stones outclassed spears, but because trust outclassed terror. He acted within his calling, using what God had trained in secret fields, and aimed at what mattered. Our obedience may look like telling the truth when a lie seems safer, asking for help when pride prefers silence, refusing compromise when fear urges surrender, or praying again when weariness says, why bother. Each act declares, this battle belongs to the Lord.

Encouragement:

Do not let size fool you. Giants fall when God fights. Your covenant God is greater than what stands before you.

Reflection:

What giant have you been measuring by size rather than by God's covenant faithfulness, and how would your next step change if the battle truly belongs to the Lord?

Notes:

_____

_____

_____

_____

Lift your eyes, what towers over you is small beside the God who stands with you.

Prayer:

Father, thank You that I need not fear what defies me when You are for me. Teach me to see every obstacle in the light of Your strength. I renounce intimidation, receive courage, and choose obedience. The battle is Yours. Steady my aim, guide my steps, and glorify

Your name. In Jesus' name, amen.

Week 35:

The Door May Not Be Closed

Introduction:

Life often feels like a series of doors, some wide open and others firmly shut. At times, we hesitate, unsure if moving forward is safe or even possible. This devotional is a gentle reminder that God is always at work behind the scenes. He sees what we cannot, and He invites us to step forward in faith even when the way seems unclear. Our hope is that as you read and reflect, these messages will encourage you to trust God's timing, recognize His faithfulness, and experience the unexpected doors He has prepared for your life. We are rooting for you, cheering on your steps of faith, and praying that God's Presence will guide and sustain you every day.

Scripture:

2 Corinthians 5:7— "For we walk by faith, not by sight."

Message:

A few years ago I approached a storefront that looked closed. Lights were dim, no movement inside, and from a distance the glass seemed almost opaque. Everything said, "Turn around." But as I drew near, the sensor caught my approach and the door slid open. That small moment felt like a parable. Some doors only open when you move toward them. From far away, the hallway of God's will can look dark. Up close, with one obedient step, the way opens.

Scripture calls this posture a walk, not a sprint or a standstill. We walk by faith, one step and then another, not by sight. Faith is not denial of reality. It is trust in a greater Reality. Israel learned this at the Jordan when the waters did not part from a distance. They parted as the priests' feet touched the river. Peter learned it when he stepped out of the boat. The surface held because Jesus had spoken. In both scenes, movement met mercy. God did not ask for heroics, only obedience, because His word, not our bravado, carries the weight of the miracle.

Closed looking seasons come to us all. Unanswered prayers, stalled applications, weary waiting, conversations that never seem to budge. Faith does not pretend those doors are bright and obvious. It remembers who holds the keys. Jesus says, "I am the way," and to a faithful church He promises, "See, I have placed before you an open door that no one can shut." If He is the Way, then the path is not a maze to master but a Person to follow. Draw near to Him, and the sensor of grace seems to wake the mechanisms we cannot see. Timing aligns, hearts soften, and opportunities appear that effort alone could never engineer.

Of course, some doors truly are closed for our good. Faith also trusts God's "no" as much as His "go," believing that a shut door can be a kind detour toward a better one. The courage we need is not recklessness but responsiveness. We listen for His voice, test our steps against His Word, invite wise counsel, and then move forward without demanding to see the whole hallway. Often the hinge turns when we risk the next right thing.

Encouragement:

Step in faith. The doors God opens respond to trust, and His timing meets you as you move.

Reflection:

Where might God be inviting you to move closer even though everything looks shut from a distance, and what would one obedient step look like today?

Notes

_____

_____

_____

_____

Take heart—what seems shut from afar may open the moment you draw near with Jesus.

Prayer:

Lord, teach me to walk by faith and not by sight. I release my need to see the whole way and choose the next faithful step. If a door is from You, open it. If it is not, close it kindly and lead me on. Align my heart with Your Word, and let Your Presence be the path beneath my feet. Amen.

Week 36:

When a Tree Falls — Living in the Direction You Lean

Introduction:

Every life is shaped long before the world ever witnesses its outcome. We often focus on the moment of impact, the crisis, the decision, the legacy, but overlook the quiet lean that led us there. Like a tree shaped over time by wind, weight, and seasons, our souls bend in the direction of our habits, desires, and daily choices. This devotion invites us to look not at how we might someday fall, but at how we are leaning right now.

Scripture:

Ecclesiastes 11:3— "...Whether a tree falls to the south or to the north, in the place where it falls, there it will lie."

Message:

A tree does not choose its landing in the instant it begins to fall. Its trajectory was written by slow forces, minute bends, deep or shallow roots, repeated winds, long summers, and hard winters. The moment of collapse only reveals what years have been forming. Ecclesiastes names that sober truth. Where it falls, there it will lie. The landing tells the story of the lean.

Our lives follow this same pattern. We do not suddenly veer into faithfulness or failure. We arrive where our daily inclinations have been quietly steering us. Some of those inclinations are subtle, an unchecked resentment, a habit of hurry, a reliance on self, a constant reaching for distraction. Others, often unnoticed by everyone but God, turn us Christward, small obediences, hidden prayers, a practiced gratitude, repeated returns to Scripture when feelings run thin. Over time these choices shape posture, and posture sets direction.

This is not meant to frighten us but to clarify the stakes of the ordinary. The world trains us to watch for dramatic moments. Wisdom instructs us to attend to daily angles. If I consistently lean toward worry, I will land in weariness. If I lean toward confession and mercy, I will land in freedom. Storms do not create our lean; they reveal it. When winds rise, roots either hold or show where soil has been neglected. And yet the gospel speaks a better word. Grace meets us not only after the fall but during the lean.

Jesus does not wait at the finish line to evaluate. He walks among the trees, speaking to the slope of our hearts now. He calls us to abide in Him, to let His words abide in us, to be rooted and built up in Him, established in the faith. That means the angle can change. In seasons of pressure, I can turn my weight toward Christ, choosing to forgive instead of rehearse offense, to pray instead of doom scroll, to rest instead of grind, to obey instead of delay. The Spirit is a wise arborist. He stakes us with truth, waters us with grace, prunes what steals strength, and strengthens what bears life.

Encouragement:

You do not have to wait for collapse to change direction. God stands ready to strengthen your roots and steady your lean now.

Reflection:

Where is your life quietly leaning, toward Christ or away from Him, and what small turn of heart would begin to realign your posture today?

Notes:

_____

_____

_____

_____

Take heart—grace can straighten what years have bent, and Christ can set your roots firm again.

Prayer:

Lord, search the hidden leanings of my life. Show me where I am bending away from You, and by Your grace, set me upright again. Root me in Your truth, water me with Your Presence, and let my life finally fall in a way that honors You. Amen.

Week 37:

Only the Guilty Need Grace

Introduction:

Grace is not for the righteous; it is for the desperate. Mercy is not for the polished; it is for the broken. If you have ever felt unqualified, unworthy, or too far gone, hear this clearly: you are exactly the kind of person Jesus came for. The gospel is not a reward for the good; it is rescue for the guilty. The moment we admit our need is the moment we become candidates for God's greatest gift.

Scripture:

Ephesians 2:8–9— "For it is by grace you have been saved, through faith, and this is not from yourselves, it is the gift of God, not by works, so that no one can boast."

Message:

Guilt is a terrible master, yet it can be a faithful messenger. When it drives me to hide or to hustle for worth, it crushes. When it drives me to Jesus, it becomes a doorway to life. Scripture is unflinching. All have sinned and fall short of the glory of God, and in the same breath it sings that all are justified freely by His grace through the redemption that came by Christ Jesus. My problem is larger than a few bad choices, and my rescue is greater than my best efforts. Salvation is not God grading on a curve; it is God giving a gift.

Jesus told a story about two men who went to pray. One performed his virtue; the other beat his chest and said, "God, have mercy on me, a sinner." Only one went home justified, the one who

109

came empty and honest. That is grace's strange arithmetic. The emptier my hands, the readier they are to receive. The Pharisee brought a résumé. The tax collector brought repentance. Which am I bringing today?

The Father's heart toward returning sinners is not suspicion but sprinting compassion. The prodigal limped home rehearsing apologies. The Father ran, embraced, and called for a robe before the speech was finished. David prayed in the same Spirit, "Have mercy on me, O God, according to your unfailing love," appealing not to his record but to God's character. There grace becomes more than doctrine. It becomes a shield against shame's accusations. I do not argue that I am good. I agree that Christ is enough.

Grace also empowers. The Lord told Paul, "My grace is sufficient for you, for my power is made perfect in weakness." God is not shocked by my shortcomings. He intends to make them stages for His strength. The past I fear disqualifies me becomes the very platform where mercy shines brightest. I can stop auditioning for love and start living from it. I can stop proving and start praising. I can step into the light where forgiveness not only covers but also renews.

So I come as I am, not to excuse sin but to expose it to the only Love strong enough to heal it. Grace meets honest guilt with undeserved favor and sends me out new.

Encouragement:

The very thing you think disqualifies you is the very reason grace exists. In Christ, you are forgiven, you are loved, you are free.

Reflection:

Am I trying to earn what God has already given freely, and do I truly believe His grace covers even me right here and right now?

Notes:

_____

_____

_____

_____

Lift your eyes—where guilt once ruled, grace now reigns.

Prayer:

Lord, I confess my need for Your mercy. Thank You that my guilt is not met with punishment but with love poured out at the cross. Teach me to step from hiding into Your light, to live not in shame but in gratitude, and to let Your grace define me, transform me, and flow through me to others. Amen.

Week 38:

The Promiscuous Grace of God

Introduction:

Sometimes God's ways challenge our expectations and stretch our understanding. His grace does not operate according to human rules. It surprises, pursues, and transforms in ways we could never predict. This devotional explores the wild, relentless, and unearned love of God that reaches into every corner of our lives, offering hope and restoration where we least expect it. May these reflections encourage you to embrace His grace fully, no matter where you are on your journey.

Scripture:

Romans 5:8— "But God demonstrates his own love for us in this: While we were still sinners, Christ died for us."

Message:

The word promiscuous sounds jarring beside grace. We usually hear it as reckless or indiscriminate, and in one sense that is why it startles us. God's grace is gloriously wide in its reach, though never careless in its aim. It goes where we would not go, sits with those we would not sit with, and invites hearts we might have written off, including our own. While we were still sinners, Christ died for us. The cross is God's public declaration that His love moves first, moves farther than we think, and keeps moving when we stop.

Consider Jesus at table with tax collectors and sinners. The religious bristled, and He replied that a physician goes to the sick.

Think of the woman caught in adultery, dragged into shame and braced for stones, who heard, "Neither do I condemn you. Go now and leave your life of sin." Grace shielded her and then set her free. Even on the cross, grace leaned toward a dying thief and opened paradise before the nails were removed. This is not tidy love. It is costly love poured out where it seems undeserved, which is the only kind we ever receive.

Promiscuous grace does not wink at sin; it wins us from it. The same Jesus who welcomes also transforms. Scripture says the grace of God teaches us to say no to ungodliness. Grace is not permissive; it is powerful. It does not pretend my past is harmless; it proclaims that my past is not final. It does not negotiate worthiness; it bestows it. Because grace is given, not earned, I cannot boast when I stand nor despair when I fall. I come back again and again to the fountain where mercy runs wider than my failure and deeper than my shame.

If the adjective troubles me, perhaps that reveals how domesticated my view of grace has become. Jesus' love scandalized the self assured and rescued the self accused. Prodigals were wrapped in robes before their rehearsed apologies finished. Elder brothers were invited to the same party they refused to enter. In both cases the Father went out, always going out, because grace refuses to keep its distance.

So I step out from self protection and step into this lavish love. I receive what I cannot repay and extend what I cannot exhaust. As that love lands, it loosens my grip on judgment and tightens my hold on Jesus, who is Himself the grace of God appearing.

Encouragement:

God's grace is not intimidated by your mess; it meets you there and leads you home.

Reflection:

Have you felt unworthy of grace lately, and what would it look like today to receive Jesus' undeserved love right where you are?

Notes:

_____

_____

_____

_____

Take heart—His grace reaches farther than your failure and holds longer than your fear.

Prayer:

Lord, thank You that while I was still a sinner You moved toward me in love. I lay down my earning and my excuses. Wash me, renew me, and teach me by Your grace to say no to what binds and yes to the life You give. Let the mercy I receive become mercy I extend. Amen.

Week 39: Remember Whose You Are

Introduction:

There are moments when insecurity creeps in, times when we feel inadequate, unseen, or unworthy. Maybe someone questioned your value. Maybe you questioned it yourself. But your identity is not determined by opinions, performance, or past failures. It is secured by one unshakable truth: you belong to Him.

Scripture:

1 John 3— "See what great love the Father has lavished on us, that we should be called children of God! And that is what we are!"

Message:

John does not invite us to glance at God's love; he commands us to see it, to stare until our hearts are shaped by what our eyes behold. The Father's love is not careful or rationed; it is lavish, poured out without reluctance on those who could never earn it. You are not merely tolerated by heaven; you are claimed, named, and placed in the family of God.

Adoption is the lens Scripture gives us for this miracle. Ephesians says we were "predestined for adoption to sonship through Jesus Christ." Adoption begins not with a child's effort but with the Father's initiative. Long before you prayed your first prayer or stumbled through your most recent failure, God had set His affection on you in Christ. The cross did not only cancel a debt; it established a new identity. Romans reminds us that while we were still sinners, Christ died for us. Grace did not wait for your holiness; it stepped into your need and said, "Mine."

Still, identity gets contested. The enemy's first strategy with Jesus was to question Sonship, "If you are the Son of God…," and the whispers have not changed. If you really belonged, why did you fall? Why do you still struggle? Why don't you feel worthy? Feelings fluctuate; sonship does not. Jesus answered with Scripture, and so must we. When accusation rises, we agree with God instead: I am a child of God, not by merit but by mercy; not by performance but by promise.

This new standing also carries new power. You are not left to maintain your identity by sheer willpower. "It is God who works in you to will and to act according to his good purpose." The Spirit inside you bear witness that you are God's child and teaches you to live like it: more free, more whole, more like Jesus. Sanctification is not you trying to become someone you are not; it is you learning to walk as who you already are in Christ. When shame tries to reattach yesterday's labels, lift your head. An heir does not negotiate belonging; an heir receives it and walks in it.

Encouragement:

You are not striving for identity; you are standing in it

Reflection:

Am I defining myself by shifting feelings and failures, or by the unchanging word God has spoken over me as His child?

Notes:

_____

_____

_____

_____

Lift your head—You are loved, you are wanted, you are His.

Prayer:

Father, thank You for calling me Your own. When insecurity speaks louder than truth, remind me who I am in Christ. Silence accusation, steady my heart, and teach me to live with confidence, not in my strength, but in the certainty that I belong to You. Amen.

Week 40:
The New Man

Introduction:

Every believer enters salvation with a past: habits, wounds, failures, and identities formed by life before Christ. But Scripture is bold in its declaration. In Christ, we are not merely improved or polished versions of our old selves; we are made new. Yet many still live as though they are chained to who they used to be. This devotion is a reminder: you are not who you were. You are who God says you are.

Scripture:

2 Corinthians 5:17— "Therefore, if anyone is in Christ, the new creation has come: The old has gone, the new is here!"

Message:

When Jesus steps into a life, He does not refurbish the old structure; He raises something entirely new upon grace's foundation. Paul does not say the old is tucked away for later. He says it is gone. Yet many of us, even after we have trusted Christ, keep reaching for the garments of yesterday. We believe God has forgiven us, but we still look into the mirror with the labels of our past taped to the glass. Heaven, however, is not confused about your identity.

Ephesians calls us to "put off the old self... and put on the new self, created to be like God in true righteousness and holiness." That language is deeply practical and profoundly freeing. We are not earning righteousness; we are wearing what Jesus already purchased.

The old self was shaped by sin's gravity and self-protection; the new self is animated by the Spirit, aligned to truth, and clothed with grace. The enemy is a historian of your failures, but the Holy Spirit is the herald of your future. The past may explain parts of your story, but it no longer defines your name.

This newness is instantaneous in identity and progressive in practice. In a moment we are transferred from darkness to light, from enemies to sons and daughters. Then, day by day, we learn to live like who we already are. The picture of Lazarus helps here. When Jesus called him from the tomb, life surged in at once, but grave clothes still clung to him until Jesus commanded, "Loose him, and let him go." In Christ, you have been raised; sanctification is the unwrapping. Old scripts like "I am just an anxious person," "I will always be angry," or "That is just who I am," are grave cloths. They do not fit resurrection life.So agree with God about you. Confess the old labels you have carried, receive again the name He speaks—beloved, clean, free—and step into practices that match your newness: truth where you once hid, mercy where you once retaliated, purity where compromise felt normal, worship where shame used to whisper. You are not destined to circle the same wilderness. Christ did not die to leave you improved; He rose so you could rise with Him.

Encouragement:

You are not defined by who you were; you are empowered by who you are in Christ.

Reflection:

What old mindsets or labels have you been carrying that Christ has already removed, and what would laying them down look like today?

119

Notes:

_____

_____

_____

_____

Take heart—grace has changed your name, and the Spirit will teach you how to wear it.

Prayer:

Lord Jesus, thank You for making me new. I renounce the old labels and lies, and I receive the name You give: redeemed, restored, and dearly loved. Teach me to put off the old and to put on the new, walking in the righteousness and holiness You have supplied. Let my thoughts, words, and choices agree with heaven's verdict over my life. Amen.

Week 41:

Freedom in Forgiveness

Introduction:

Holding on to resentment is like carrying a weight that saps strength, clouds thinking, and dims joy. God's call to forgive is radical because it invites us to release that weight and step into freedom. Forgiveness is not excusing wrong or pretending the hurt didn't happen; it is choosing grace over bitterness and trusting God with justice and healing.

Scripture:

Colossians 3:13— "Bear with each other and forgive one another if any of you has a grievance against someone. Forgive as the Lord forgave you."

Message:

Paul situates forgiveness inside the wardrobe of the "new self." Right before this verse he tells us to clothe ourselves with compassion, kindness, humility, gentleness, and patience. Forgiveness is the thread that binds those garments together. "Forgive as the Lord forgave you" is not mere moral advice; it is a gospel-shaped command. We forgive out of the surplus we have received.

How did the Lord forgive us? Completely, willingly, and at great cost. Earlier Paul says God "forgave us all our sins" by canceling the record of debt and nailing it to the cross (Colossians 2:13–14). Jesus does not minimize evil; He bears it. He does not keep a ledger waiting for repayment; He pays it Himself. His forgiveness removes our guilt and loosens shame's grip, restoring communion where estrangement reigned. To forgive "as" Christ forgave is to draw from that same fountain: I release the debt not because it was small, but because His grace toward me is greater.

Forgiveness is not the same as reconciliation, nor is it the erasure of wise boundaries. Reconciliation requires two willing hearts; forgiveness can begin with one. Boundaries may still be necessary to guard what is good. Yet in God's economy, forgiveness is the turning point for the one who was wounded: the refusal to let bitterness be the narrator of your story. It is an act of faith, placing the gavel back in God's hand, entrusting Him with what you cannot resolve, and inviting the Spirit to heal what anger cannot.

How do we take this from command to practice? Start by naming the wound honestly before God. Next, release the debt to Him, sometimes in a single decisive prayer, often in repeated prayers as the ache resurfaces: "Father, because You have forgiven me in Christ, I choose to forgive." Ask the Spirit to bless the one who harmed you, not to deny the pain, but to dethrone revenge. Where appropriate and safe, pursue steps toward peace; where not, keep walking in the freedom of a heart unshackled. Over time, forgiveness reshapes our inner world—softening pride, strengthening compassion, and making space for joy to return. Because it is rooted in Christ's finished work, forgiveness is never wasted, even when feelings lag behind the choice.

Encouragement:

Forgiveness is not weakness; it is the Spirit's strength releasing your heart to live in God's peace.

Reflection:

Is there someone, another person or yourself, you need to forgive so you can step out from under the weight and into Christ's freedom?

Notes:

_____

_____

_____

_____

Take heart—grace loosens what bitterness binds, and Jesus leads you into peace.

Prayer:

Lord Jesus, thank You for forgiving me fully and freely. I bring You the wounds I carry and the debts I keep. By Your grace, I release them into Your hands. Heal what is broken, guard my heart with wise love, and lead me in whatever peacemaking is right and safe. Teach me to live as one who is truly free. Amen.

Week 42:

In Everything, Give Thanks

Introduction:

Life moves in seasons: times of joy, times of struggle, times of waiting. In every season, God invites us to cultivate gratitude. Gratitude transforms our perspective, helping us notice His faithfulness even when circumstances seem difficult, and it anchors our souls in His unchanging goodness.

Scripture:

1 Thessalonians 5:18— "Give thanks in all circumstances; for this is God's will for you in Christ Jesus."

Message:

Paul's command is both bracing and beautiful: give thanks in all circumstances. He does not ask us to pretend that every circumstance is good; he calls us to locate God's goodness within them. Gratitude, then, is not a thin layer of cheerfulness spread over pain; it is a deep orientation toward God's character—His steadfast love, wise providence, and unfailing Presence. Psalm 107 begins with a refrain that steadies the heart: "Give thanks to the Lord, for he is good; his love endures forever." When circumstances shift, that sentence does not.

Thanksgiving is a discipline of sight. Left to ourselves, we naturally fixate on what is missing, what is frightening, what did not go as planned. Gratitude trains the eye to notice manna on the ground, mercies new in the morning, and the quiet ways God has been carrying us. It begins with the simple, breath in our lungs, a meal received, a word of encouragement, then widens to the profound: forgiveness that cleanses shame, guidance that arrives at the right hour, strength that meets us at the end of our own. The practice does not deny sorrow; it refuses to grant sorrow the final editorial control.

Philippians 4 links thanksgiving with peace. We present our requests to God "with thanksgiving," and in the very act of entrusting them, His peace stands guard over heart and mind. Gratitude opens the hands that worry keeps clenched. It reminds us that our story is held by a Father who knows what we need and has pledged Himself to our good in Christ. Even unanswered prayers are reframed: if the door remains closed, gratitude remembers that God's "no" is never careless and His timing is never late.

Gratitude is also profoundly relational. We give thanks to God, and we express thanks to people. When we name the graces we have received from others—a listening ear, a shared burden, a faithful Presence—we echo the generosity of God and strengthen the bonds of community. Thanksgiving begets encouragement; encouragement begets courage.

Encouragement:

Gratitude does not shrink your pain; it enlarges your awareness of God's faithful love within it.

Reflection:

Where can you intentionally give thanks today—even in a hard place—and how might that act of gratitude reshape your perspective?

Notes:

_____

_____

_____

_____

Lift your eyes—there is more mercy in your day than you have yet noticed.

Prayer:

Lord, teach me the holy habit of thanksgiving. Open my eyes to Your daily mercies, from the smallest gifts to the greatest grace in Jesus. When worry presses in, help me to remember, to name, and to give thanks, trusting Your goodness and faithfulness in every season. Amen.

Week 43:
The Power of God's Promises

Introduction:

We live in a world crowded with promises—offers that expire, intentions that fade, and guarantees written in disappearing ink. God's Word is different. His promises do not wobble with headlines or hinge on human strength. They rest on the unshakeable character of the One who speaks.

Scripture:

2 Corinthians 1:20— "For no matter how many promises God has made, they are 'Yes' in Christ. And so through him the 'Amen' is spoken by us to the glory of God."

Message:

Paul roots our confidence where it belongs—in Christ. Every promise of God finds its resounding "Yes" in Jesus. When we wonder if God will be faithful, we look not to our feelings but to the finished work of the Son. The cross and the empty tomb are heaven's exclamation point over every word God has spoken.

"God doesn't make casual statements, He makes covenants." He does not dabble in declarations; He binds Himself in steadfast love. From Abraham's starry sky to Jeremiah's new covenant, from Isaiah's suffering servant to Ezekiel's new heart, God's Word is promise-shaped, and Jesus is its fulfillment. "His promises are not wishes, intentions or hopeful words; they are guaranteed realities anchored in His character." If He has said it, He will do it; if He has spoken it, He will bring it to pass, in His timing, by His power, for His glory and our good.

Still, we live between promise and fulfillment, where impatience nips at faith. Here Scripture trains our posture. Abraham "did not waver through unbelief regarding the promise of God, but was strengthened in his faith" (Romans 4:20). Strength came as he considered not the obstacles but the One who promised. Peter says God's "very great and precious promises" enable us to participate in the divine nature (2 Peter 1:4)—promises are not merely comfort; they are formation. They pull our lives into alignment with God's heart.

Practically, we can hold a promise three ways. We remember it— rehearsing what God has said until it steadies our steps. We pray it, letting our "Amen" rise through Christ, not to twist God's arm but to train our trust. We live it, making choices today that agree with the future He has declared. When fear whispers scarcity, we live generously because He promised to supply. When shame drags its feet, we walk forgiven because He promised to cleanse. When the way seems dim, we keep moving because He promised to guide.

God's promises are not escape hatches from hardship; they are anchors in it. They do not remove the storm, but they keep us from drifting. With that assurance, we turn our faces toward the future and let our hearts say a confident, Christ-shaped "Amen."

Encouragement:

The One who promised is faithful; your "Amen" in Christ ties today's obedience to tomorrow's certainty.

Reflection:

Which specific promise from God do you need to remember, pray, and live today, and how will agreeing with it change your next step?

Notes:

_____

_____

_____

_____

Take heart—His promises hold fast, and He holds you.

Prayer:

Faithful Father, thank You that every promise finds its "Yes" in Jesus. Train my heart to remember Your Word, my mouth to pray it, and my life to live it. Where I'm tempted to doubt, anchor me in Your character. Let my "Amen" bring You glory and shape my steps today. Amen.

Week 44:

The Gift of Listening

Introduction:

In a world filled with constant noise and unrelenting demands, the ability to truly listen has become rare. We often hear words without absorbing them, respond before understanding, and rush to speak our own perspective. Yet God calls us to a higher standard: to listen attentively, to Him and to others. Listening is more than hearing; it is an act of love, a gift that fosters connection, understanding, and peace.

Scripture:

James 1:19— "Everyone should be quick to listen, slow to speak and slow to become angry."

Message:

James' instruction lands with gentle urgency: be quick to listen. Let listening lead. When listening leads, anger loses momentum and careless words lose their grip. Listening, in the biblical sense, is not passive reception but active love, an honoring of the image of God in the one who speaks. It requires humility to admit we don't yet see the whole picture and patience to let another person finish before we begin.

We learn this first with God. "Be still, and know that I am God" invites us to lay down the frantic need to fill silence and to make room for His voice. Scripture opens our ears; prayer trains our attention; silence clears the static so the Spirit's gentle nudges can be discerned.

Elijah did not find God in wind, earthquake, or fire, but in a low whisper. Many of God's most tender directions arrive not as thunder but as a quiet clarity that surfaces when we wait. Listening to God shapes how we listen to people; His kindness in our depths becomes gentleness at our lips.

Attentive listening to others is a spiritual practice that heals. Proverbs warns that answering before listening is folly; love moves slower. To truly listen is to receive more than content, it is to receive a heart. It is noticing what is said and what is withheld, the sigh between sentences, the wound beneath the argument. Jesus modeled this again and again: He listened to the woman at the well until her thirst surfaced; He heard blind Bartimaeus over the crowd's noise; He drew out the disciples on the Emmaus road before opening the Scriptures to them. His questions dignified people; His responses restored them.

Practically, listening begins with small obediences, pausing before replying, asking one more curious question, reflecting back what we heard to ensure we understood, and inviting the Spirit to govern our tone. It means resisting the urge to fix too quickly and offering Presence before solutions. In conflict, listening becomes a bridge; in grief, it becomes a shelter; in everyday conversations, it becomes a seedbed for trust. As we make space in our ears and schedules, we make space for grace to flow.

Encouragement:

Listening well is a generous gift, offered freely, it grows understanding, quiets anger, and opens doors for grace.

Reflection:

Where is God inviting you to practice deeper, more attentive listening, toward His voice or toward someone in your circle who needs to be heard?

Notes:

_____

_____

_____

_____

Slow down, lean in—God often speaks most clearly when we listen most carefully.

Prayer:

Lord, teach me to listen with a still heart and an open mind. Help me hear Your voice above the noise and offer my attention generously to others. Let my questions be kind, my responses measured, and my Presence a channel of Your peace. Amen.

Week 45:

Living a Thankful Heart

Introduction:

A thankful heart is more than a seasonal sentiment; it is a lifestyle. When gratitude shapes our thoughts, words, and actions, we experience God's peace more deeply and become living testimonies of His goodness to those around us.

Scripture:

Colossians 3:15–17— "Let the peace of Christ rule in your hearts, since as members of one body you were called to peace. And be thankful. Let the message of Christ dwell among you richly as you teach and admonish one another with all wisdom through psalms, hymns, and songs from the Spirit, singing to God with gratitude in your hearts."

Message:

Paul's vision for a Christian life is not grim duty but rich, resonant gratitude. "Let the peace of Christ rule in your hearts." The verb suggests an umpire, a decisive arbiter. When anxiety and irritation compete for the final call, Christ's peace steps in to rule, and on the heels of that ruling comes a simple command: "And be thankful." Gratitude is not an accessory to peace; it is its ally. As thanksgiving rises, worry lowers. As praise is voiced, perspective clears.

This gratitude grows where "the message of Christ" dwells richly. The gospel is not a guest who drops by; it is a resident who fills the house. When Christ's word moves from the shelf to the center, read, prayed, sung, obeyed, our inner world changes tone. Teaching and admonishing become wise and gentle because they spring from mercy received. Worship becomes the natural language of a heart steeped in grace: psalms rehearsing God's faithfulness, hymns lifting the cross and resurrection, Spirit breathed songs giving voice to today's mercies. Gratitude is the music underneath it all, tuning the soul to God's goodness.

Psalm 100 invites us to "enter his gates with thanksgiving and his courts with praise." Thanksgiving is not merely a response once we feel joyful; it is a doorway into joy. We do not wait for perfect conditions to give thanks; we bring thanks into imperfect conditions and find that God meets us there. Philippians 4 deepens the promise: present your requests to God with thanksgiving, and His peace will garrison your heart and mind. Gratitude does not deny grief; it discovers grace within it. It does not ignore need; it brings need to a Father whose love endures forever.

Gratitude also moves outward. A thankful heart notices and names the good in others: encouragement that steadies a friend, a quiet act of service that reflects Christ, a word of appreciation that knits community. In a world fluent in critique, thanksgiving is a countercultural witness. And it is practical: begin the day with a simple thanks, rehearse God's kindness at mealtime, end the evening recounting one trace of His faithfulness. As these habits take root, Colossians 3:17 comes alive, "whatever you do... do it all in the name of the Lord Jesus, giving thanks." Gratitude becomes the signature under every task, the refrain beneath every step.

Choose, then, to live with a thankful heart; let Christ's peace rule, let His word dwell, and let your life sing with a gratitude that points beyond you to Him.

Encouragement:

A life rooted in gratitude cultivates joy, welcomes peace, and keeps you awake to God's steady goodness.

Reflection:

How could gratitude reshape the way you experience God's Presence and provision today; what will you thank Him for right now?

Notes:

Begin with thanks—joy often follows right behind.

Prayer:

Father, fill my heart with thankfulness. Open my eyes to daily mercies, seen and unseen, and let the message of Christ dwell richly in me. May Your peace rule my heart, and may my words and actions reflect Your goodness, drawing others to give thanks to You. Amen.

Week 46:
Hope That Lasts

Introduction:

The end of the year often brings reflection on joys and struggles, victories and losses. Yet in the midst of looking back, God invites me to look forward with hope. Hope is more than wishful thinking; it is a firm confidence in the promises of God, anchored in His faithfulness and illuminated by the gift of Christ. As the season of Christmas reminds me of the arrival of my Savior, it also reminds me that His hope is present now, powerful, and enduring.

Scripture:

Romans 15:13— "May the God of hope fill you with all joy and peace as you trust in him, so that you may overflow with hope by the power of the Holy Spirit."

Message:

Hope lives best where trust is practiced. Paul's blessing does not begin with my resolve but with "the God of hope," the Source who fills, steadies, and overflows my life. Joy and peace do not rise from perfect circumstances; they grow as I actively trust Him. Hope, then, is not fragile optimism; it is the Spirit's power holding me when answers are partial, timing feels slow, and endings are still unwritten.

I think of how God has led through other uncertain seasons. When I could not see the next turn, His word became a lamp to my feet, not a floodlight to the horizon, but enough light for the next step. That is often how hope works: quiet, persistent, arriving with the morning mercies I did not earn. The same Lord who placed a star in Bethlehem's sky still guides by His Presence, nudging, comforting, correcting, and reminding me that nothing in my story has slipped beyond His reach.

This hope is rooted in God's unchanging character. He is faithful when I am faltering, near when I feel numb, sovereign when the world trembles. Because Jesus has come, my future is not chained to my past; because Jesus still reigns, my present is not ruled by my fears. Even the waiting rooms of life can become sanctuaries where hope learns endurance and trust grows deep roots. When sorrow lingers, hope does not scold; it sits beside me and lifts my eyes to a Savior who has overcome the world.

Hope also changes how I live toward others. Filled by the Spirit, I become a conduit, not a container, carrying encouragement into anxious rooms, practicing patience where irritation once lived, choosing generosity when scarcity shouts. The more I rely on God's hope, the more I notice its quiet evidences: the timely word, the unexpected provision, the peace that does not make sense on paper. And as the year folds to a close, I am invited to step forward not with bravado, but with a holy expectancy, because the One who holds tomorrow is already there.

So I breathe, trust, and ask the God of hope to fill me again, until what He pours in begins to overflow.

Encouragement:

God's hope is not temporary; it endures and overflows. Let it anchor your heart and color every step ahead.

Reflection:

Where in my life do I need to let the hope of Christ replace fear, worry, or doubt, and what would trusting Him in that specific place look like today?

Notes:

_____

_____

_____

_____

Take heart—His hope holds fast, and His hand is already in your tomorrow.

Prayer:

Lord, you are the God of hope. Fill me with Your joy and peace as I trust You. Quiet my fears, steady my thoughts, and cause Your hope to overflow in me by the power of the Holy Spirit. Lead me into the new days with confidence in Your faithful love. Amen.

Week 47:

Peace in the Storm

Introduction:

Life's storms are inevitable. Sudden trials, unexpected losses, and shifting circumstances can leave even the strongest hearts shaken. Yet Jesus offers a peace that the world cannot replicate, a peace that does not depend on circumstances but on His Presence. It is the calm in the chaos, the steady hand in turbulent waters, and the quiet confidence that no matter how fierce the storm, we are not alone.

Scripture:

John 14:27— "Peace I leave with you; my peace I give you. I do not give to you as the world gives. Do not let your hearts be troubled and do not be afraid."

Message:

Jesus promises peace on the eve of the cross. The Upper Room is thick with uncertainty, questions about departure, betrayal, and what comes next. Into that anxiety, He does not hand His disciples a strategy; He bequeaths them a gift, "my peace." This is not the fragile ceasefire the world calls peace, conditional, temporary, easily revoked. It is the settled wholeness of Christ Himself shared with those who belong to Him, the fruit of His Presence and the pledge of His Spirit.

Storms will come. They arrived for the disciples on the Sea of Galilee as winds roared and waves climbed the boat's sides. When they shook Jesus awake with, "Don't you care if we drown?" He rose and spoke to the weather as if calming a child, "Quiet, be still." The sea obeyed, but notice the order: before the storm changed, the Savior stood. His nearness reframed their fear. Peace is not the absence of trouble; it is the Presence of Christ, God with us, stronger than what surrounds us.

Psalm 46 sings the same reality, "God is our refuge and strength, an ever present help in trouble." The ground may heave, but the God who holds it does not. Faith does not deny the storm's force; it denies the storm's final word. When panic surges, we anchor in what we know: The Lord is sovereign, the Lord is near, the Lord is good. His peace is active, guarding hearts and minds, steadying steps, clarifying choices when confusion threatens to scatter them. Isaiah calls it perfect peace for the mind stayed on God; Paul calls it a peace that surpasses understanding, keeping watch like a sentinel over anxious thoughts.

Abiding makes this peace tangible. When I slow my breathing and turn my attention to Jesus, when His word is the voice I let shape my inner weather, when I place my concerns into His hands again and again, a different atmosphere settles. Circumstances may not shift yet, but I am no longer tossed in the same way. Out of that inner calm flows an outward witness. Peace received becomes peace shared, gentle words for a fearful friend, prayer that lifts another's burden, Presence that sits quietly with the hurting like a lighthouse on a hard shore.

So hear the gift again, "my peace I give you." Let your heart loosen its grip on control and take hold of Christ.

Encouragement:

His peace does not depend on the storm; it rests on the Savior, and He is with you.

Reflection:

What storm in your life most needs Jesus' peace right now, and how will you choose to abide in Him rather than be led by fear in that place today?

Notes:

_____

_____

_____

_____

Take courage—His peace stands taller than the waves and nearer than the wind.

Prayer:

Lord, thank You for Your unshakable peace. In the winds that rise and the waves that threaten, fix my gaze on You. Guard my heart and mind, steady my steps with Your Presence, and teach me to carry Your calm into the lives of others. I trust Your hand more than I fear the storm. Amen.

Week 48:

Joy in the Journey

Introduction:

Life is not a straight path. It is a journey filled with twists, valleys, peaks, and unexpected turns. Often, we focus so intently on the destination that we overlook the lessons, growth, and blessings along the way. God calls us to embrace joy not just at the finish line, but throughout the journey itself.

Scripture:

James 1:2–4— "Consider it pure joy, my brothers and sisters, whenever you face trials of many kinds, because you know that the testing of your faith produces perseverance."

Message:

Joy in the journey is not a denial of difficulty; it is a defiant confidence in God's nearness and purpose. James invites us to "consider," to make a deliberate assessment, that trials, though unwelcome, can become the very workshops where faith is forged. Joy, then, is not a mood that drifts in with good weather; it is a choice anchored in what we know: testing produces perseverance; perseverance matures us so that we become complete, not lacking anything. The hardships that threaten to hollow us out can, under God's hand, make room for deeper strength and steadier hope.

Joseph's story traces this truth across years, not days. Sold by brothers, enslaved in a foreign land, falsely accused, forgotten in prison, each chapter looked like detour and loss. Yet Scripture keeps saying, "The Lord was with Joseph." God's Presence did not remove every setback; it redeemed them. In time, the very path that seemed to ruin him positioned him to bless many. What others meant for evil, God wove for good. Joy along such a road is not giddy optimism; it is the quiet conviction that God is neither absent nor idle, that He is working even when the page looks dark.

Joy also grows where gratitude takes root. "This is the day the Lord has made; let us rejoice and be glad in it" is not a call to pretend; it is a call to perceive. When I begin to notice daily mercies, strength to take the next step, a friend's timely word, an unexpected provision, a Scripture that lands as if written for today, joy finds oxygen. Gratitude turns ordinary moments into altars where I remember that God has not let go of my hand.

This joy does not shrink our witness; it strengthens it. A life that keeps trusting God through trial speaks loudly in a world that measures happiness by circumstance. Joy in the journey says Christ is enough in plenty and in want, on the peaks and in the valleys, in the waiting and in the arriving. It does not deny tears; it carries them to the One who bottles them. It does not erase questions; it rests them on promises. And as we take the next faithful step, we discover that joy travels with us, because Jesus does.

Encouragement:

Joy is not only at the destination; it grows with every faithful step you take with Jesus today.

Reflection:

Where in your current journey can you choose to see God's hand and embrace joy, even in the midst of trial, and how might that choice shape your next step?

Notes:

_____

_____

_____

_____

Take heart—He walks with you, and His joy is strong enough for the road ahead.

Prayer:

Lord, teach me to find joy in the journey. Open my eyes to Your Presence in the hard places and Your kindness in the small graces. Form perseverance in me, anchor my heart in Your promises, and let Your peace and contentment fill me as I walk with You. Amen.

Week 49:

Living Like You're Loved

Introduction:

Many of us know in our minds that God loves us, yet our hearts still move cautiously, as if His affection were fragile and could be lost. We pray timidly, strive for approval, and measure ourselves by our best or worst day. But the love of God is not conditional or scarce; it is lavish, steady, and glad to draw near. The gospel does not stop at "forgiven." In Christ, we are fully embraced, endlessly cherished, and eternally valued.

Scripture:

1 John 4:16— "And so we know and rely on the love God has for us. God is love. Whoever lives in love lives in God, and God in them."

Message:

There is a world of difference between agreeing that "God loves me" and actually relying on His love. John links knowing with relying because love is meant to be leaned on, not admired from a distance. When I live as one who is loved, I stop auditioning for affection that I already have. I bring my real self to prayer, the anxious thoughts, the mixed motives, the half-finished obedience, because love has already made room for me. I am not entering a throne of evaluation but a throne of grace.

God's love is not cautious around my weakness. While I was still a sinner, Christ died for me. He did not wait for worthiness. Adoption was His idea, not my achievement, so my identity is not on a probationary period. The Father's delight is not a reward for flawless performance; it is the atmosphere in which I learn to walk. As this settles, shame loses leverage. I confess quicker because love has already decided to stay. I obey deeper because love produces desire where fear once drove duty. Joy rises, not from self-confidence, but from being rooted and established in a love that will not let me go.

Living loved reshapes ordinary days. I speak more gently because I am no longer fighting to be seen. I forgive more freely because I am no longer collecting debts to prove my value. I risk holy courage because failure can no longer tell me who I am. Even suffering is reframed. I may not understand the path, yet I am not unloved on it. The cross is my forever proof. The Spirit within me is my daily assurance. The Father's heart is my home.

So I choose to rely. I let His love carry my weight in this very moment. As I do, that love not only holds me; it also sends me to love others with the same steadiness I am receiving.

Encouragement:

You are not loved a little; you are loved completely. Let that love set the tone of your day.

Reflection:

Do you live as someone striving for love, or as one confidently walking in it, resting in the certainty that you are wholly cherished by God?

Notes:

_____

_____

_____

_____

Lift your head—You are deeply loved, and His love makes you brave.

Prayer:

Father, thank You that Your love is vast, unchanging, and near. Teach my heart to rely on it. Quiet the lies that I must earn what You freely give. Let Your delight reshape my thoughts, steady my steps, and overflow through me to others. In Jesus' name, amen.

Week 50:
The Gift of Christ

Introduction:

Christmas is often painted with twinkling lights, bustling stores, and the joy of giving and receiving gifts. Yet beneath the celebrations lie the heart of the season, the gift of Christ. Unlike any other gift, He was not wrapped in paper or tied with ribbon; He was wrapped in humility and laid in a manger. God's greatest gift is not something we can hold in our hands, but Someone who transforms every heart willing to receive Him.

Scripture:

Luke 2:10–11— "But the angel said to them, 'Do not be afraid. I bring you good news that will cause great joy for all the people. Today in the town of David a Savior has been born to you; he is the Messiah, the Lord.'"

Message:

The angel's first words are the ones my heart needs most: do not be afraid. Into a night field and an ordinary world, heaven spoke joy that would not be confined to the privileged few but poured out for all people. The gospel's headline is not a demand; it is a declaration. Good news has arrived, and it has a name. Jesus is not merely a symbol of hope; He is the Savior who brings hope with Him.

How He came still arrests me. No palace and no procession. The eternal Son chose a borrowed manger and the quiet company of shepherds. This is the pattern of our God: glory clothed in humility, majesty wrapped in swaddling cloths. The manger does not diminish His worth; it reveals His heart. He did not wait for us to climb to Him; He came down to where we are, entering the world's poverty to lift us into the riches of His grace.

To receive this gift is more than acknowledging a story; it is welcoming a Person. The Child in the straw is the Lord of my days. When I open my life to Him, the Bethlehem scene moves from history to habitation. Christ dwells within. Peace begins to replace panic. Forgiveness cleanses what guilt could not. Purpose sprouts where weariness once grew. Joy becomes more than sentiment; it roots in the certainty that God is with us and for us.

The shepherds did not keep the news to themselves. They hurried to see, then returned glorifying and praising God. True receiving becomes holy telling. Each kindness, each word of blessing, each moment of worship echoes that first announcement into our own dark fields: do not be afraid, a Savior has come. Christmas is not a brief sparkle; it is an abiding light. The gift given once in Bethlehem keeps giving, guidance for the confused, comfort for the broken, mercy for the sinner, strength for the faint.

Encouragement:

The gift of Christ is not fleeting. He is with you now, bringing joy, peace, and hope that endure.

Reflection:

Are you living as one who truly receives Christ, allowing His Presence to shape your thoughts, choices, and relationships each day?

Notes:

_____

_____

_____

_____

Take heart—Emmanuel has come, and His light is still finding us.

Prayer:

Lord, thank You for the gift of Your Son. I treasure Jesus above every other good thing. Let His light fill my heart, steady my steps, and shine through my words and actions. Make my home and habits a manger where Your Presence is welcomed and Your love made known. Amen.

Week 51:

Faithful Through Every Season

Introduction:

As the year comes to a close, it is natural to look back at triumphs and trials, laughter and tears, what bloomed and what broke. Through every chapter, one truth has held: God's faithfulness has not wavered. His love has surrounded us, His mercy has met us, and His grace has carried us through every season, regardless of circumstance.

Scripture:

Lamentations 3:22–23— "Because of the LORD's great love we are not consumed, for his compassions never fail. They are new every morning; great is your faithfulness."

Message:

Faithfulness is often quiet. It does not always arrive with fireworks; it arrives with sunrise. Jeremiah wrote these words while looking over ruins, not roses. Yet from the rubble he could still say, great is Your faithfulness. God's steadfast love had not resigned, His compassions had not run dry, His mercies were already on their way with the dawn.

Looking back across the months, most of us can name places where we felt unseen or uncertain, days we carried more than we thought we could, moments when we wondered if the road would ever level out. And yet, here we are. Still standing. Still held. That endurance is not proof of our strength; it is evidence of His faithfulness. Every provision that arrived at the right time, every word of comfort that landed like a lifeline, every prayer answered loudly or quietly, these were the footprints of a God who does not leave.

God's faithfulness also reorders our future. Plans may have shifted and some doors closed. His character does not move with the market or the calendar. The plans of His heart stand firm, which means our lives are not at the mercy of chance. They rest in the hands of a Father whose wisdom is perfect and whose love is relentless. His mercies are not leftovers from last year. They are fresh baked every morning, enough for today, and they will be enough tomorrow.

So we respond with gratitude that names His goodness, trust that loosens our grip on control, and mercy that mirrors His heart toward others. We can step into new days without bravado, with a settled courage. The God who carried us will keep carrying us. The One who guided us will go ahead of us. The Lord who forgave us will keep forming Christ within us.

Encouragement:

His steadfast love meets you where you are, renews your strength, and gives real hope for the road ahead.

Reflection:

Where do you most need to trust God's faithfulness today, and what would relying on His new every morning mercy look like in that place?

Notes:

_____

_____

_____

_____

Take heart—His mercies will meet you again with the morning.

Prayer:

Lord, thank You for Your unending faithfulness. When my heart is anxious, steady me with Your compassions that never fail. Teach me to rest in Your mercy, to remember Your goodness, and to walk boldly into each new day, confident in Your love and care. Amen.

Week 52:

Anchored in His Promise

Introduction:

As this year long journey of reflection, encouragement, and spiritual growth comes to a close, we remember the One who has carried us through each week. Joys and trials have both had their say, but God's promises have not wavered. The hope we confess is not fragile sentiment. It is anchored in the faithfulness of God Himself.

Scripture:

Hebrews 10:23— "Let us hold unswervingly to the hope we profess, for he who promised is faithful."

Message:

Hope in Scripture is not wishful thinking dressed in religious language. It is confidence rooted in God's character. The writer of Hebrews calls us to hold unswervingly, to grip with steady hands a hope fastened to Someone trustworthy. We do not anchor our souls to outcomes we cannot control. We anchor to a God who cannot lie. Promises are only as strong as the One who makes them, and the One who has spoken over our lives is faithful.

Looking back over the year, we can trace His faithfulness in threads both bright and quiet. Provision arrived at the right hour. Guidance came like a lamp to our feet. Comfort settled when words failed. Psalm 33:4 affirms what experience has whispered, the word of the Lord is right and true, He is faithful in all He does. Even in stretches where prayers felt delayed and the road turned in ways we did not expect, His mercy met us with the morning and His steadfast love kept us from being consumed.

Holding hope does not ignore pain. It refuses to let pain be the final narrator. Faith and hope travel together. Faith trusts the Promiser, hope waits for the promise. The cross guarantees God's heart toward us. The empty tomb guarantees His power for us. Because Jesus lives, our future is not tethered to our past, and our present is not ruled by fear. The God who sustained us yesterday will shepherd us tomorrow. The covenant love that has carried us will carry us still.

So we tighten our grip where weariness would loosen it. We rehearse what God has said until our hearts remember. We align plans and priorities with His truth, expecting His faithfulness to intersect ordinary days. As this series closes, we step forward without bravado and with a steady courage. The God who promised is faithful, and His faithfulness will be our stability in the season ahead.

Encouragement:

God's faithfulness is your anchor and His hope your compass. Walk boldly into what is next, confident in His love.

Reflection:

Which promise of God do you most need to hold today, and how will clinging to it strengthen your heart for the year ahead?

Notes:

_____

_____

_____

_____

Take heart—He who promised is faithful, and His mercy will meet you with the morning.

Prayer

Lord, thank You for Your unshakable promises. As this year closes, teach me to hold hope unswervingly. Steady me in every detail, meet me in every trial, and gladden me in every joy. Anchor my life in Your truth and guide my steps by Your grace. Amen.

Series Conclusion:
Walking Forward in Faith

Introduction:

Over the past fifty-two weeks you have walked through encouragement, reflection, and God's Word. You have tasted His faithfulness, grace, love, and guidance. Each devotion was a stepping stone meant to strengthen your heart, sharpen your perspective, and deepen your life with Christ. Today we pause to notice the tapestry of lessons, the gentle nudges of the Spirit, and the clear moments that have drawn you closer to Him.

Scripture:

Philippians 1:6— "Being confident of this, that he who began a good work in you will carry it on to completion until the day of Christ Jesus."

Message:

This journey has pressed a true and steady promise into our hearts. God's work in you is ongoing, tender, and intentional. Each weekly focus was more than reading. It was an invitation to encounter Jesus and to let His Spirit shape your thoughts, actions, and affections. When you learned to wait with hope, to use gentle words, to witness by the Spirit's power, and to abide in the True Vine, you were not collecting ideas. You were receiving formation.

Think of the moments you were stretched to forgive, to trust, to rest, or to step forward in faith. These were not random tasks. They were threads in a single fabric. Philippians 1:6 assures us that the good work God began is the work He carries forward. Every prayer answered, every quiet insight, every step of obedience has been part of His faithful hand at work within you.

Perhaps this year surfaced struggles you did not expect. Doubts rose. Fears spoke. Even there the lessons of grace, mercy, and hope held firm. God's faithfulness does not move with circumstance. His love remains constant. His promises endure. His Presence stays near. Every reflection and every moment of stillness has been a reminder that you are seen, loved, and equipped to walk with courage.

As this series closes, receive it as a launch rather than an ending. Carry these truths into ordinary days. Let gratitude frame your vision. Let hope guide your choices. Let faith move your feet toward God's purpose. Spiritual growth does not stop. It unfolds. One step. One prayer. One act of love at a time.

Encouragement:

You are not the same person who began this journey. God has met you, shaped you, and equipped you. Walk forward in faith, hope, and love, confident in His Presence and His promises.

Reflection:

Which lessons from this devotional year rest deepest in your heart, and how will you carry them into each new day?

Notes:

_____

_____

_____

_____

Take a moment and listen. Sometimes life becomes clear in the stillness.

Prayer:

Lord, thank You for guiding me through this devotional journey. Help me remember what You have taught me. Teach me to live fully in Your grace and to trust Your faithfulness in the days ahead. Let these truths shape my heart, my choices, and my life, so that every step brings glory to You. Amen.

www.ingramcontent.com/pod-product-compliance
Lightning Source LLC
Chambersburg PA
CBHW030259130626
46549CB00002B/605